THE
INDIVIDUALISM
OF
DONALD TRUMP

SIMON LENNON

The Individualism of Donald Trump
Non-Fiction (Political Biography, Commentary and Opinion)
Published by Pine Hill Books
Copyright © 2021 by Simon Lennon
ISBN 978-1-925446-44-9 (electronic)
ISBN 978-1-925446-45-6 (paperback)
50,000 words
Cover image: The White House, Washington, D.C.

To ordinary Americans

CONTENTS

1. NATIONALISM

Patriotism is emotion. Nationalism is policy.

Nationalism is also carrying that policy into effect, safeguarding or bettering a nation and people. Sometimes, nationalism requires work.

Patriotism is easy because emotions are easy, even if expressing patriotism can provoke problems from people hostile to a country and people. Patriotic duty can be much harder, requiring action. Nationalism is more akin to patriotic duty than simply patriotism.

Nationalism makes the nation a person's identity, her people the person's compatriots, and their interests one in the same. Nationalism brings and keeps compatriots together, treating each other as their own.

Patriotism is for everyone. It can do most good among rich and powerful people.

Nationalism is for every person making decisions affecting one's compatriots. It is for every elected official, bureaucrat, and judge exercising authority over others.

It is for every consumer choosing which product to buy or person to hire. It is for every business owner choosing who to employ and where to conduct manufacturing and other operations.

Rich and powerful people make more of those decisions than other people make. Their decisions affect more people and affect people more. Poor and powerless people cannot do much to help or harm rich and powerful people, but rich and powerful people can do a lot to help or harm everyone else.

When rich and powerful Americans gave up their nationalism through the second half of the twentieth century, America divided. She became more and more deeply divided.

Divisions separated the rich and powerful from ordinary Americans. They separated people living in coastal cities from heartland towns and cities they flew over or drove past without looking out their windows.

There were Democrats and Republicans, but on the issues that mattered, the two parties agreed. Aside for the occasional reprieves, by the early twenty-first century, America's major political parties had both abandoned nationalism. They had both become self-serving globalist.

The richest and most powerful Americans allowed ordinary Americans the opiate of patriotism: the joys of waving Old Glory, the pride of singing *The Star-Spangled Banner*, hand on heart. They might well have sniggered under their breath, but they let patriotism persist. They might even have worn a little Old Glory on their lapel pins whenever sitting or standing before television cameras or other audiences. Patriotism was a marketing tool for candidates seeking political office or businesses selling consumer products, lovingly holding hands without talk of reality.

While ordinary Americans found solace in patriotism, American governments, bureaucrats, and courts quietly pulled away practical policies to protect them: to put Americans first, or even second or third, when Americans' interests conflicted with other people's interests. Practical measures would have been nationalism.

Purchasing cheaper product, American businesses established or utilized factories in other countries, especially Mexico and China. They closed or neglected American factories, without thought of Americans losing their jobs and those Americans' communities.

Rich and powerful Americans welcomed immigrants minding their children, washing their laundry, and filling other people's jobs. Diversity depressed wages.

Globalism was making rich people in rich countries richer, while rich Americans spoke as if there was something virtuous about them cutting their costs and improving their profits. Whether through trade or immigration, they were proud to have brought up millions of people of other races from poverty, or from one good lifestyle to a better lifestyle. Critics were only concerned that other races had not improved their wealth and health still further.

The living standards of ordinary white Americans stagnated or fell backwards. In 2012, the Harvard School of Public Health estimated that the life expectancy of white American women without high school diplomas declined by five years from 1990 to 2008. Their life expectancy was ten years less than that for white American women with college degrees or better. Through that period, white American men without high school diplomas lost three years of life. Their life expectancy became thirteen years less than that of white American men with college degrees or better.

Ironically, rich and powerful people with no thought of others dismiss nationalism as selfish. Without nationalism, capitalists are no less generous with other people's lives and money than are socialists.

Diversity breaks down society. Race and religion divide people the world over. Immigration let them divide American citizenry too.

"It's not surprising, then," said Barack Obama of suffering Pennsylvanians, at an event in San Francisco in April 2008 raising funds for his presidential campaign, "they get bitter, they cling to guns or religion or antipathy to people who aren't like them or anti-immigrant sentiment or anti-trade sentiment as a way to explain their frustrations."

People not believing in nations do not appreciate how much nations protect people, especially but not only the working and middle classes. People without religion do not understand religion. "He's a drop dead atheist, absolutely," commentator Bill Maher would say of Obama, complimentarily, in conversation with Jon Stewart on *The Daily Show* in June 2014.

In July 2008, Obama addressed two hundred thousand Germans in Berlin as "a proud citizen of the United States and a citizen of the world." He spoke for America's self-appointed global elite, many of whom might not have felt rich and powerful, but being financially comfortable, they were rich and powerful aside America's poor and powerless. "The walls between the countries with the most and those with the least cannot stand. The walls between races and tribes, natives and immigrants, Christian and Muslim and Jew cannot stand."

Obama was not so disparaging of Muslims and Jews clinging to their religion as he was of rural Pennsylvanians clinging to theirs. Neither was anyone else.

Countries outside the West were not taking immigrants from other races and tribes as America was. They could keep their walls.

In an America where every other race freely asserted itself and its religion, white people were forbidden from defending themselves and their religion. People whose lifestyles had declined and who witnessed their cultures dissipating and heritage being eroded were increasingly being told they had a privilege being white. Living in wobbly timber shacks with no chance of a job beyond itinerant work, while the country increasingly elected, enriched, and empowered people of other races often because of their race, white privilege was hard to feel.

Expressing American nationalism took courage. American nationalism was racism because America was still primarily white, but nothing had become worse than white people expressing racism. Most Americans could not afford to do so.

The few political candidates expressing nationalism did so in the most modest of terms. Patriotism remained rife, but without the policies to substantiate it, the patriotism of political candidates was simply politicking. Caring about white people would be racist.

None of it was unique to America, but was common around the West. Americans were more demonstrative than others with their patriotism because Americans were more demonstrative than others about everything, but even that was starting to wane.

What was unique to America, from the time in June 2015 that he announced his candidacy for the Republican Party nomination for the presidential election due in November 2016, was Donald John Trump. Born in Queens, New York in 1946, Trump was a billionaire businessman and television personality who had never held elected office. No person had previously become president without political or military experience.

Simply declaring America to be great would have been patriotism. Recognizing that she was no longer great took something more. Trump's promise to *"Make America Great Again"* was patriotic for wanting America to be great again. It was nationalistic for promising to put patriotism into effect.

It was also nationalistic for recognizing the reality in which America stood. Nationalism is always a matter of reality: recognition of human nature and circumstance.

Although not the first use of the phrase, Ronald Reagan in his successful 1980 presidential campaign used the slogan *"Let's make America great again."* It played to the claim that incumbent President Carter had weakened America, but also came after the pains of the Vietnam War and President Nixon's Watergate scandal through previous administrations.

Bill Clinton used the phrase in his successful 1992 presidential campaign and in a radio commercial for his wife Hillary's unsuccessful campaign in 2008. It was a phrase for a candidate from the political party not currently in office.

In December 2011, Trump explained the reason he might someday become a candidate for president. "I must leave all of my options open because," he said, "above all else, we must make America great again."

Voters interpret political slogans in the context of everything else that candidates say. Reagan saw American greatness fighting communism.

"When Mexico sends its people," said Trump at the launch of his presidential campaign in June 2015, "they're not sending their best... They're sending people that have lots of problems, and they're bringing those problems... They're bringing drugs, they're bringing crime, they're rapists, and some, I assume, are good people."

Trump's promises varied widely throughout the campaign, but they included various measures to cut legal and illegal immigration. Trump associated Islam with terror, so that he spoke explicitly or implicitly at various times through his campaign of banning some or all Muslims from America.

Economic activity was not a matter of numeric data but people's livelihoods. American nationalism wanted trade that put Americans to work manufacturing product to sell to other countries, instead of trade that enriched already rich Americans in offices funding the development of factories elsewhere. Trump promised measures to revive American manufacturing.

He spoke of other matters too from a nationalist viewpoint, but none mattered as trade and immigration mattered. Trump's pitch was a return to nationalism and a rejection of the globalism that had increasingly dominated elite Western thinking since World War II. He promised globalization that put America first instead of submitting her to the rest of the world.

So divided was America, the rich and powerful remained unaware of those divisions. They remained unaware not just of the tens of millions of white Americans from whom they had been divided over decades, but also the people of other races from whom they had always been divided.

Instead, America felt united. All the people they knew agreed with them. All the people on television and in the newspapers agreed with them, at least on the television stations they watched and in the newspapers they read. Everyone they knew welcomed immigrants, perceived no link between Islam and terror, and saw free trade as a godsend. The immigrants they met were polite, at the office or serving them meals.

Trump's comments and promises related to immigration attracted the most vitriolic condemnation. People comfortably divided from Christian white Americans were appalled at talk of division with Muslims and other immigrants.

Rich and powerful people considered America united when ordinary Americans believed them that running down their country was for their own good, delivering America to others. If suffering Americans were unhappy, they had silently to accept it. So did Americans simply wanting to keep the country their forebears made, but who had no say in giving America away.

Divisions between people cannot be healed until they are aired. Trump's candidacy gave hope for that healing.

The 2016 election was a chance for rich and powerful Americans to recognize the worsening divisions by race, class, and religion across America. Instead, critics accused Trump of creating those divisions, as if they would not have otherwise been there.

Trump did not create divisions. He revealed divisions already there.

He centered his campaign upon people neglected for decades. "I love the poorly educated," Trump told a rally in Las Vegas in February 2016. It was nationalism unabashed.

The only people that America's elite hated more than Trump were his supporters. Everything he was, they were, without his excuse of campaigning for president.

In a speech in New York in September 2016, Democrat nominee Hillary Clinton expressed the attitude of America's elite to people they never met: the division between rich and poor white Americans that rich Americans wanted. "You know," she said, "to just be grossly generalistic, you could put half of Trump's supporters into what I call the basket of deplorables."

Her audience laughed. It applauded.

"Right?" she asked.

Again, her audience laughed. It applauded.

"They're racist, sexist, homophobic, xenophobic, Islamophobic – you name it – and unfortunately, there are people like that, and he has lifted them up. He has given voice to their websites that used to only have eleven thousand people, now have eleven million. He tweets and retweets their offensive hateful mean-spirited rhetoric. Now, some of those folks, they are irredeemable, but thankfully, they are not America."

Hers was the same disparaging of ordinary Americans as from Obama eight years earlier. There were eight more years of invented bigotries with which to malign them.

Emboldened by Trump, his supporters mocked those who mocked them. Defying the insults made against them, they proudly called themselves Deplorables.

Trump gave a voice to people who had been voiceless for generations. People with voices hated him for it.

To elite Americans enjoying their comfortable routines, complainants did not know what was good for them. Dismissing tens of millions of Americans, Trump's critics dismissed the role of policy and messaging in his support.

Unable to understand the lure of nationalism, their explanations for Trump's support included a personality cult around him. Without a royal family, Americans had long made much of their presidents. The adoration could be like cults of personality, as it was with Barack Obama, although he was far from the first president almost sanctified.

Where emotion counted more than reason, political commentator Chris Matthews told MSNBC television viewers in March 2008 that "I felt this thrill going up my leg" as Obama spoke. "I don't have that too often."

"Steady," said fellow commentator Keith Olbermann.

Obama and Trump espoused hope, to a country in need of hope. Rich white people saw Obama as the man to save the world. Poor white people saw Trump as the man to save America.

The adoration of some people for Trump was no different to the adoration of some people for Obama, but they were different people. Among white people, Obama was a hero to people who did not need heroes or heroines. Trump was a hero to people who did. Trump promised to champion people who in living memory had not enjoyed a champion.

Obama's adoration came from powerful celebrities, journalists, and commentators accustomed to seeing themselves on screens. News, television, and other media expressed them.

Trump's adoration came from powerless people, many of

whom had also voted for Obama, if without that adoration. They needed signs and flags.

Rich people mocked rickety homes and rusting cars adorned with banners and stickers supporting Trump, as if to say that supporting Trump was a symptom of the same failings that made them poor. Nothing did more to affirm their contempt for working-class white people. Middle-class lawns decked with Trump signs remained unnoticed.

Unfamiliar with promises like those that Trump made, there arose talk of Trump-ism, but it was never only Trump. There was no Trump-ism.

Supporting compatriots is nationalism. Trump defended American nationhood.

James Carville first became prominent for his role in Bill Clinton's presidential campaign of 1992. In 2020, Carville expressed as well as anyone the ideological opposition to Trump.

"The idea is not just to defeat Trump," Carville told interviewer John Melendez in May 2020. "You have to defeat Trump-ism. You have to defeat the idea that the United States of America is a place and not an idea."

By reducing America to an idea, Carville denied America's existence, but whatever idea Carville thought was America was not unique to America. American ideas are common across the West. Some American ideas occur outside the West, too.

Reducing a country to an idea denies that country's people, cultures, and industry. That is globalism.

Carville seems not to have reduced other countries to being ideas. Globalism only erases Western countries.

America is a place. All countries are places, with borders, cultures, and people.

Central to Trump's support was that, unlike other figures of his time, his rhetoric always affirmed America existed and her existence was beneficial: America had been great and could be great again. There are many factors in play in any democratic election, but in all the circumstances of 2016, Trump exuded enough nationalism to win.

Espousing nationalism did not make Trump a nationalist. Like Carville and others among his opponents, Trump did not understand the nationalism that would have made America's interest his interest, American his identity, and fellow Americans his compatriots. Instead, Trump's nationalism was an individualist nationalism, limited to the nationalism that benefited him personally.

Trump enjoyed the benefit of other people's nationalism. Nationalism benefits people.

Rich and powerful people need the nationalism of others, even if too few rich and influential white people still realized it. Poor and powerless people knew they needed nationalism.

A nationalist would have focused upon his people and delivered upon policy. Through his presidency, Trump did little more than promise nationalism, but in an era when other American political figures did not promise nationalism, Trump's promise almost won him re-election.

With nationalism, Trump could have helped heal America's divisions. He could have been re-elected in 2020.

Especially through the last months and weeks of his presidency, Trump proved himself a minimal nationalist. He had brought divisions to light not to deal with them, but to exploit them.

Trump did not mirror the nationalists who supported him. He mirrored more the individualists who opposed him.

2. INDIVIDUALISM

The antithesis of nationalism is not simply globalism. It is individualism.

Trump was a product of the era in which he lived: the West's Age of Individualism. He was much like other rich Americans, but without their veneers of politeness.

For a nationalist American, America and individual Americans matter. For an individualist, only individuals matter, but only he or she really matters.

People committed to a cause, religion, or people do not need applause. They do not need a crowd before them in a stadium or among computer screens. Attention is only useful as a means of attaining something, such as winning elections, when the important work begins.

For individualists, attention can be its own reward. Individualism is narcissism.

Trump might have only ever wanted attention. "I can be the most famous man in the world," he told his aide Sam Nunberg at the start of the 2016 presidential contest, according to Michael Wolff's 2018 book *Fire and Fury*. Trump referred not to being president, but to the presidential campaign he could run.

He was already a rich and famous narcissist, among a plethora of rich and famous narcissists, in what had become a country of narcissists. People liked nothing better than declaring on social media their opinions for all to read and hear. Other people photographed themselves, with blurs behind them that might or might not be somewhere significant.

The only narcissism people condemn is other people's narcissism. Other people should be as fixated with them as they are.

Being adored is best. Being despised suffices. Only being unnoticed dissatisfies.

Initially favored to win the Republican Party nomination for the 2016 election was former Florida governor Jeb Bush: a son to

President George H W Bush and a brother to President George W Bush. Two presidencies had made the Bushes a political dynasty, in a country familiar with dynasties. A third family member closer than cousin becoming president would be unprecedented.

Jeb Bush offered continuity with past presidencies, ensuring that nothing important changed. The perfect foil to Trump's anti-establishment campaign, Bush never escaped Trump's belittling of him as "low energy."

Belittling political competitors is one thing, in a democratic contest. Competing political candidates have competing personal interests.

Belittling compatriots who are not political competitors is brazenly nasty. While nationalists in the national good might pull down people threatening their country, they do not recklessly brawl with their compatriots.

People committed to fulfilling their objectives are not easily distracted. Nor are nationalists focused on their countries and compatriots.

Trump was distracted by criticisms that a nationalist focused upon America, or even a candidate trying to win an election, would have ignored. Most notable in 2016 was his longstanding feud with comedienne Rosie O'Donnell.

In 2006, Trump part-owned the Miss Universe Organization. Miss U.S.A. was alleged to have visited public bars while under the legal age to do so and to have used illegal drugs, but Trump decided not to strip Tara Conner of her crown. "Tara is going to be given a second chance," Trump told a news conference at the time.

Speaking afterwards on the television program *The View*, O'Donnell condemned Trump's decision. Instead of arguing the reasons Conner should have lost her crown, she assailed Trump personally.

Nationalists debate the merits of an issue. Individualists make personal attacks.

If there was substance in Trump's replies, it became lost in counter abuse just as personal as O'Donnell's abuse had been. In spite of the wealth to which he was born, Trump had the instincts of a streetfighter, not a gang member, but a solitary fighter. A gang member might have been more nationalistic.

Whatever response O'Donnell's comments warranted in 2006, Trump remained unduly fixated with their feud ten years later. So was she, but if her objective was to undermine his campaign for president, she had a reason to be fixated. O'Donnell might not have been a nationalist, but in 2016, she was not a candidate for president.

Like a lot of Trump's insults, his insults of O'Donnell could entertain, but it is not in the nature of a nationalist to be so bitter towards a compatriot. Nationalism focuses a person's mind upon compatriots to help them, especially the compatriots who need help, not to fight them. Nationalism is not belittling the rich and powerful, but helping the poor and powerless.

Nationalism connects compatriots, joining men, women, and children of a nation together. That makes nationalists naturally nice to their compatriots, although conflicts arise.

Nationalist men are gentlemen, at least in the West. Nationalist women are ladies, especially in the West. What being a lady or a gentleman entails varies by time and place. Gentlemen apologize whenever apologizing is right.

Nationalists might lack connection with people of other nations, but individualists lack connection with anyone. They can be awful to anyone, unless they have an interest in being polite.

Trump rarely recognized that interest, standing apart from other horrible people by being nakedly horrible. Being rude and obnoxious made him seem genuine, amidst poll-driven politicians with public-relations politeness.

If Trump-ism were just abuse without purpose, then that Trump-ism lost in 2020, but it never really won in 2016. Abuse served Trump well in 2016 because it set him apart from past presidents and other candidates as much Republican as Democrat. Past presidents had been pleasant, presiding over America's decline. Amidst their awful actions decade after decade, there were more bases upon which to judge people than niceness.

Ordinary Americans, tired of being unable to speak freely, loved Trump's candor, even if they disliked his coarseness. Trump could have maintained every policy position he took without uttering abuse, but his brashness made him appear an agent for change, giving credibility to his promises. Policy prevailed, especially concerning trade and immigration.

By Election Day 2016, Trump probably was the most famous man in the world. No more complete an individualist ever stumbled into the White House. "So I sort of thought I lost,"

Trump told a rally in West Allis, Wisconsin in December 2016, of his response to exit polls after the election, "and I was okay with that."

Trump's public squabbles continued into his presidency, where he had more powerful forces against him than Rosie O'Donnell. *"The Campaign to Impeach Trump has Begun,"* declared *The Washington Post* newspaper the day of Trump's inauguration.

No American, let alone a president, was subject to more relentless abuse and mockery than was Trump after he dared win the 2016 election, but he brought much of it upon himself. The greatest force against Trump was himself. He made impeachment easy, twice.

"You're really big," special counsellor Kellyanne Conway told Trump when trying to dissuade him from a course of action, according to Howard Kurtz's 2018 book *Media Madness.* "That's really small."

Nationalism is the big picture, as are the forces against it. Individualism is the smallest of pictures.

Trump's celebrity critics were often just as petty minded as he was. They too were individualists. Individualism is petty.

Nationalism makes pettiness fall away. Nationalists might brawl with nations. Individuals brawl with individuals.

Trump did not convey a sense of duty. He did what he wanted to do, and always had.

Of all the many virtues that America had lost, none was more precious than duty. Duty comes from nationalism, inviting not just sacrifice, including the ultimate sacrifice, but labor. Duty is able-bodied people striving for the sake of their families, people, and nations.

Nationalists work as hard as their national interests require, according to their skills and capacities. That work varies in nature and degree through different stages of life and in different situations. Working people do not have to work hard, if they work well.

Critics accused President Reagan of working too little, especially near the end of his presidency. In response, he joked of retirement after the White House being little different to working. Reagan liked to joke.

President Clinton spent long hours in the Oval Office. He was not always working.

The satirists' summary of President George W Bush's plan during his re-election bid in 2004 to deal with the debacle in Iraq was that he was working hard on a solution. It did not help. America would have fared better if Bush worked less hard in his first term, if that avoided the Bush-led and Blair-led invasion of Iraq.

Before his election, Trump was right in much of his political and economic commentary. When he had the chance to act upon it, he squandered his opportunity.

Trump's nationalism was the nationalism that recognized problems affecting his nation, and especially the poor and powerless among his people. Thus he recognized what America needed to do to become great again. He lacked the nationalism to carry it through: to do all he could in office to put nationalism into effect, to make America great again.

Nationalists want to aid their countries. Trump preferred to talk and tweet.

From Twitter came new uses of the noun and verb: tweet. Twitter and other social media had long let Trump bypass the mainstream media to communicate directly with people. The spelling errors, sloppy language, and poor grammar provided him with authenticity. (Trump's typing errors have generally been corrected in this book.)

"Without the tweets, I wouldn't be here," Trump told the *Financial Times* newspaper in April 2017. "I have over one hundred million followers between Facebook, Twitter ... Instagram." By the 2020 election, Trump had almost ninety million followers on Twitter.

Away from the cameras, it was easy to imagine Trump's tenure in office sitting lonely in the dark, tweeting words that millions of people read and to which thousands reacted. Most people could not do anything about America's troubles than talk, tweet, or write about them, but the president could do something. There was much chatter, but little real activity.

When Trump thought about issues, he was very insightful, but he too rarely thought about issues. He was smart but lazy.

Human beings need rest from work to function best when they do work: the Biblical one day off in seven. That is time with family and friends, playing games and sport, and attending church.

"*Can you believe that,*" tweeted Trump in October 2014, "*with all of the problems and difficulties facing the U.S., President Obama spent the day playing golf. Worse than Carter."*

CBS News White House correspondent Mark Knoller kept a tally of Obama's games of golf. *"Pres Obama ending 2016 same way he began it,"* Knoller tweeted at the start of January 2017. *"With round of golf at @MCBHawaii. 64th round in 2016 and 333rd as pres."*

Trump played almost as many rounds of golf in one term as Obama played in two terms. *"President Trump arrived at Trump International Golf Club in West Palm Beach, Florida, at 9:26a on Wednesday,"* tweeted CNN correspondent Jim Sciutto at the end of 2020. *"Since taking office, this is the 426th day Trump has spent at one of his properties and the 313th day he's gone to one of his golf clubs, according to CNN's count."*

This was not a man striving to save America. It was a man striving to sink golf balls.

Trump spending so much time playing golf and tweeting during his presidency did not need to be an issue, if everything was happening that needed to happen. It was not.

When he did something, Trump issued fine-sounding executive orders, which produced inadequate effect. He supported proposals and legislative bills that never became law. Trump had the intellect and office to do more than he did.

Presidential achievement required time in the quiet of rooms and offices with people with power to act. Trump could have lobbied or lobbied more congressmen and women upon legislative changes, resolving any logjams. He could have lobbied other world leaders in America's interest. He could have followed up with bureaucrats the implementation of his executive orders.

Playing golf with people is not lobbying them. It is playing golf.

So great a mission as making America great again requires work, with forces pointed against her like the vested interests against which Trump railed in 2016. Trump might have felt patriotism, but not the patriotic duty for which men and women are willing to strive and, to whatever degree the circumstances of the time require it, sacrifice for their countries and compatriots. Trump would make America great again, to the extent that he was not inconvenienced.

Most obviously through the pandemic of 2020, Trump's time playing golf and tweeting became like the Emperor Nero proverbially fiddling while Ancient Rome burned. If playing golf was supposed to convince Americans to behave without thought of the pandemic, then playing golf never looked like risking a person becoming infected. Not all Americans could play golf.

It was hard to see Trump sacrificing anything through his presidency, although he gave up his presidential salary. A man playing golf and tweeting instead of working should not draw a salary.

From the late eighteenth century through Victorian times, Britain did not pay her members of parliament. Parliamentary service was a public duty, reserving it to the aristocracy without need of income. Proponents of paying parliamentary salaries stressed the importance of helping working men into Parliament, but it did not happen until 1911. Even then, the salary of four hundred pounds a year was the same as that of a junior clerk in the civil service. The less nationalist Britain became through the twentieth century, the greater the incomes that politicians approved themselves being paid.

America had no tradition of public duty. The Constitution required the president to be paid a salary.

Congress voted to pay the first president, George Washington, a salary of twenty thousand dollars per annum. A massive sum in 1789, it amounted to two percent of the federal government budget.

"If I'm elected president," said Trump campaigning in New Hampshire in September 2015, "I'm accepting no salary, okay?" His gesture demonstrated the sacrifice he said he was making by seeking the presidency, but not needing the income also affirmed the wealth he possessed. "That's not a big deal for me."

Trump remained what he had become in adulthood: a showman; a marketer, marketing himself. With the fanfare it needed, Trump in office donated his presidential salary every quarter to various government departments.

Presidents Hoover and Kennedy had also been wealthy enough to donate their presidential incomes to charities and charitable causes. Kennedy's charities included the United Negro College Fund and the Cuban Families Committee.

Trump also remained what he had been raised to be: a New York property developer. In October 2020, *The Washington Post* newspaper reported that Trump hotels and resorts had charged the American government two and a half million dollars in hosting official functions during his presidency.

Much of his time, Trump spent at his property Mar-a-Lago in Palm Beach, Florida. With a president in residence, people paid up to two hundred thousand dollars for membership at the resort, said journalist Laurence Leamer on *Weekends with Alex Witt* in January 2021. Leamer wrote the 2019 book *Mar-a-Lago*, subtitled *Inside the Gates of Power at Donald Trump's Presidential Palace.*

The problem was not the showmanship of Trump's campaign in 2016, or even that the show never stopped. The problem was his presidency being so little else, but a show. The West was consumed by image over reality.

Many of Trump's achievements would have occurred whoever was president, driven by Congress and bureaucrats. Other achievements could have been those of any Republican president, reversed by the next Democrat.

Trump began reversing the rest before he left office. On his last day in Washington, Trump revoked the executive order that he made eight days after taking office that barred former officials from lobbying for five years after leaving his administration.

The order had been a small step towards draining the self-serving swamp that Washington had become. Revoking the order proved that the swamp remained.

Trump's show had become repetitious. He could be like a re-run, but some shows fare better in syndication than others fare.

Good deeds remained, as all presidents do some good and some bad. Trump's presidency probably did more good than harm, which probably could not be said of any other Republican president or some Democrat presidents since Eisenhower. Trump might have aided America's poor and vulnerable more than other presidents of late, but those most in need of nationalism from their elected officials suffered most by his shortcomings.

Trump did not make America great again. Nor did he really try. He talked and tweeted, as showmen do, between rounds of golf.

The man with a keen sense of nationalist policies to assist ordinary Americans had limited interest in implementing them. That America was only a short way towards becoming great again at the end of Trump's presidency attests to his failure to work hard enough or to work better. Without nationalism, it is not clear that Trump working harder would have helped, for a showman elected the accidental president who never ceased being a showman.

Convincing his supporters that he fought for them, beyond talking and tweeting, might have been Trump's greatest achievement, but he lost the 2020 election for his self-serving individualism through his term in office. Voters do not vote for other people's individualism. Without nationalism, they vote for their individualism.

It had seemed that Trump so preferred golf and Twitter to working that, if he lost re-election in 2020, he might simply shrug his shoulders and return to his clubs, courses, and computers. He could blame his loss upon something external to his performance in office and continue life unchanged.

The alternative view was that Trump so hated losing and so loved attention that he would fight his loss. The latter view proved correct.

3. GLOBALISM

Outside the West, nationalism and other tribalism remain the norm from one race to another, from one country to another, from one regime and political system to another. Nationalism does not need any more defending or advancing there, but it desperately needs defending and advancing in the West.

The first duty of nationalists is protecting their people's lives, excluding from their countries outsiders who might harm them. When there is doubt, as there often is, safeguarding their people prevails over indulging outsiders, even safeguarding outsiders.

Globalists indulge the rest of the world. Their people do not interest them.

Individualists indulge themselves. Globalism and individualism meld together because globalists keep themselves safe, along perhaps with their family and friends, without interest in the rest of their countrymen and women.

When individuals realize that safeguarding themselves requires safeguarding their countries, they turn to nationalism. Individualists recognizing the harm that globalism does to them personally turn to an individualist nationalism: defending their countries to the extent they see their self-interest.

Trump's talk of nationalism might not have been sincere. His rejection of globalism probably was sincere, but only to the extent of his individual interests.

President Carter was an old-style Democrat. In 1979, during the Iranian hostage crisis, Carter ordered all Iranians in America on student visas to report to American immigration officials or face possible deportation. A federal judge initially held the attorney-general's order giving effect to Carter's order unconstitutional, before the ruling was reversed on appeal. It led to almost sixty thousand Iranian students registering, more than four hundred being deported, and five thousand voluntarily leaving America.

In 1980, among other measures, Carter ordered administration officials to "*invalidate all visas issued to Iranian citizens for future entry into the United States, effective today. We will not reissue visas, nor will we issue new visas, except for compelling and proven humanitarian reasons or where the national interest of our own country requires. This directive will be interpreted very strictly."*

Carter's measures were not simply intended to protect Americans at home. They were sanctions intended to pressure the Iranian government into releasing Americans held hostage in Tehran.

In 2015, Trump linked Islam to terror, as Islamic terrorists did but the West did not. After the Muslim terror attacks in Paris in November 2015, killing a hundred and thirty people, Trump called for a database of Muslims in America. After the Muslim terror attack on an office training event and Christmas Party in San Bernardino, California in December 2015, killing fourteen people, Trump issued a statement that he was *"calling for a total and complete shutdown of Muslims entering the United States until our country's representatives can figure out what is going on."*

Ordinary Americans welcomed his ideas. Officialdom was appalled.

There were several differences between Trump's proposals and Carter's orders thirty-five years earlier. Carter's orders were tied to a country, Iran. Trump's proposals were tied to a religion, Islam.

The differences ran deeper than that. They ran to the differences between nationalist America in 1980 and the globalist West in 2015.

In 1980, America acknowledged Iranians' hostility towards her. In 2015, the West refused to acknowledge any other race or religion's hostility towards white people, or towards each other.

Trump's Muslim ban went through several variations before his election. It went through more variations in office, to weave its way through a judicial network that considered religious discrimination worse than Islamic terror; no American judge had been killed.

Trump honored his promise, probably as far as he legally could, although he banned only a small minority of Muslims worldwide and from a minority of Muslim countries, being those from which most terrorists came. Like Carter's humanitarian exemptions, Trump's ban had exemptions, perhaps to get through American courts or perhaps on economic grounds.

Trump's ban seemed not to harm his approval among Muslims, who also suffered from Islamic terror. In November 2018, the Pew

Research Center reported that thirteen percent of American Muslims considered themselves Republican, which was a small, statistically insignificant, increase from the eleven percent of 2007 and 2011.

"I will end the Muslim ban on day one," Democrat nominee Joe Biden told the Million Muslim Votes Summit hosted by Emgage Action in July 2020.

Trump did not make an issue of Biden's promise in 2020, perhaps trying to appeal to Muslims or to white people aghast at restrictions upon Muslims, but they did not vote for Trump anyway. He might have taken for granted the memories and support of Americans concerned about Islamic terror. He might have grown distant from their concern.

Globalism is not only a matter of indulging terror. It stains every field of American activity.

Before Trump, Republican presidents led the way with globalism, not simply for Reagan's fixation with defeating Soviet communism in the 1980s. "Out of these troubled times," George H W Bush told a joint session of Congress in September 1990, "...a new world order can emerge." With Obama, Democrats caught up.

Trump understood the stakes. "The fundamental question of our time is whether the West has the will to survive," he asked, in a speech in Warsaw, Poland in July 2017. "Do we have the confidence in our values to defend them at any cost? Do we have enough respect for our citizens to protect our borders? Do we have the desire and the courage to preserve our civilization in the face of those who would subvert and destroy it?"

Valuing truth, classic liberals would have criticized Trump's exaggerations and lies. Respecting free speech and independent thought, classic liberals would have criticized Trump's lack of civic discourse to other viewpoints. Both criticisms, classic liberals would also have made of Trump's opponents.

Classic liberals would have nevertheless supported many of Trump's policies. Confident in Western Civilization, cultures, and people, they would not have kowtowed to other races and religions. They knew that countries were places, with cultures, and people. They were nationalists and racists.

The West needed someone to break from her trajectory since 1945. Trump set himself up as the defender of Western Civilization for those who wanted it defended. It might have been nothing more than a title he awarded himself, part of the show, but it was the promise of nationalism, amidst a West with little promise.

Rich and powerful America was better placed than any other country to be an engine of revival, setting an example for other Western countries. Trump was most popular among people who supported America, Western Civilization, and white people. That included nationalists around the West, primarily in Eastern Europe. It also included people of other races and nations who did well from America and appreciated her: who recognized that American nationalism was of benefit to their races and nations too. Nationalism does not need to be at other nations' expense. Racism does not need to be at other races' expense.

Trump was most opposed by those most opposed to America, Western Civilization, and white people. Among the foes of American nationalism were nationalists from races, nations, and religions opposed to America.

Other foes of American nationalism were American globalists and individualists. Oblivious to the rest of the world, senior American political, media, and other figures, especially in New York, Washington, and Los Angeles, only knew people like them, dismissing American nationalism. They knew no one supporting Trump, so when Trump won the 2016 election, they needed an explanation.

Few Americans could have supported Trump, they were certain. Few non-white people could have supported him, they were just as certain.

That left white people from other countries. The most significant other white county in the world, and America's rival since World War II ravaged other European countries even more so, was Russia.

Russia had racial and religious minorities, but she rejected globalism around the turn of the century. She no longer rejected Western Civilization as she had done under communism through most of the twentieth century. Inconceivably to Western elites, Russia returned to nationalism. By 2016, Russia had become the West's most forceful defender.

Other East European countries had also rediscovered nationalism and staunchly defended Western Civilization, but Russia was bigger and louder. Most Americans could not name the leaders of other East European countries, but they knew Russian president Vladimir Putin. For Americans enamored with all other races and religions, Putin was their particular anathema, their *bête noire*, until Trump.

Russia was the rationale that Trump's opponents in America and elsewhere gave for Trump's election win they could not otherwise comprehend. They were certain that Putin delivered it.

Special Counsel Robert Mueller's investigation into Russian involvement in the 2016 election concluded in March 2019. Mueller reported that the Russian Internet Research Agency had conducted a social media campaign supporting Trump's candidacy and attacking Hillary Clinton's candidacy, although Russia's campaign was tiny aside Trump and Clinton's campaigns.

Russian intelligence hacked and released damaging material from the Clinton campaign and various Democratic Party organizations. Electronic mail exposed the Democratic National Committee favoring Hillary Clinton over Senator Bernie Sanders' in their campaigns for the Democratic Party nomination.

People who voted for Trump knew the reason they voted for him. Russia had nothing to do with it.

In August 2020, William Evanina, the head of the National Counterintelligence and Security Center, issued a statement saying that he was particularly concerned about Russia, China, and Iran seeking to influence the 2020 election. China wanted Biden to win. Russia preferred Trump. Russia associated Biden with the "*anti-Russia 'establishment'*" in America.

There was never so extensive an investigation into Chinese or Iranian interference in the 2016 election, which would have been similarly inconsequential. Investigating China or Iran would be racist.

America's elite only worried about Russia. People who dismissed rational concerns about Muslims as Islamophobia could not see the irrationality of their fears: their Russo-phobia.

Eager to submit to other races and religions, along with no end of international bodies and agreements, they were singularly defiant towards nationalist Russia. Globalist Americans willing to intervene in other countries' affairs proved aghast at Russia intervening in theirs.

American nationalism and Russian nationalism had the common interest of Western Civilization. If Trump had been a nationalist defending Western Civilization as he claimed to be, he would have found common ground with Russia in international affairs. Instead, apparently determined to prove that he owed his success in 2016 to no one but himself, the individualist Trump never drew upon the ally upon whom he could have drawn. Saving the West was a task for many countries.

The global mindset that erased American borders not only diminished American people, cultures, and manufacturing. It invited the American military to expand, also to America's cost.

Following World War II, American presidents sent Americans to fight foreign wars, joining them or starting them. They reflected rich Americans' willingness to let poor and middle-class Americans suffer and die to help everyone else.

American nationalists do not want Americans expending blood. They especially do not want Americans dying in other people's wars, in which America had no interest.

The Syrian Civil War began in 2011. "*We should stay the hell out of Syria,*" Trump tweeted in June 2013, "*the "rebels" are just as bad as the current regime. WHAT WILL WE GET FOR OUR LIVES AND $ BILLIONS? ZERO.*"

In April 2017, Trump's elder daughter Ivanka Trump tweeted: "*Heartbroken and outraged by the images coming out of Syria following the atrocious chemical attack yesterday.*" Shortly afterwards, Trump ordered the bombing of Syria. Trump's son Eric told the *Daily Telegraph* newspaper that he believed Ivanka influenced Trump's decision.

There was no surer sign of the distance between Trump the extraordinary candidate and Trump the typical president than the bombing of Syria. Hours before it happened, referring to Syrian president Bashar al-Assad, Hillary Clinton told the Women in the World conference in Manhattan that "we should have and still should take out his airfields and prevent him from being able to use them to bomb innocent people and drop Sarin gas on them." The month after he took office, President Biden also bombed targets in Syria.

Nevertheless, aside from that relapse, Trump did not start or join any foreign wars. Nor did he end any.

Philip Rucker and Carol Leonnig's 2020 book *A Very Stable Genius* described a meeting between Trump, the Joint Chiefs of Staff, and others at the Pentagon in July 2017. "You're all losers," Trump told America's military leaders. "You don't know how to win anymore."

Instead of winning, America's military leaders liked to spend money, grow the military bigger and better, and send soldiers to fight. Yet Trump appointed many former military personnel.

America's massive military expenditure suited America's military leadership and defense contractors. Other countries, many of them rich countries, freeloaded.

Like foreign aid, military spending in defense of other countries continued adding to America's massive national debt. In 2016, Trump campaigned upon making America's allies contribute more to the costs of their defense.

Wealthy South Korea's payments pursuant to the Korea Special Measures Agreement of 1991 fell far short of America's costs stationing military personnel there. Trump in office made some moves towards South Korea paying more, in defense from communist North Korea.

Trump's dealings with North Korea were like most of his presidency. There were abuse, threats, and promises, evolving into some sense of negotiation by the president proud of his negotiation skills.

North Korean Supreme Leader Kim Jong-un learned what others learned: Trump did not carry through with his threats. Bravado proved to be bluff. Talk gave way to nothing.

Kim continued doing what he had always done. Trump lost interest, easily bored, and moved on to talk and tweet of other things. In August 2019, Trump's random fantasies included America buying Greenland.

In December 2019, Trump created the United States Space Force. "We rebuilt the United States military," he said in his January 2021 farewell speech, "created a new force called Space Force that, in itself, would be a major achievement for a regular administration. We were not a regular administration." If it had been a regular administration, Americans might have believed that Space Force was real.

Outside the West, countries' foreign policies put their countries first. That is nationalism.

Like President Wilson at the outbreak of World War I, Trump described his foreign policy as the nationalist America First. Only in the globalist West would such a policy be controversial, although Trump's foreign policy was probably more Trump First, when he or Ivanka was interested.

Trump was much like Kim Jong-un. Both were practically synonymous with their countries.

In spite of their propaganda otherwise, no leaders are more individualistic than communist dictators. They can afford to be. Leaders of democracies cannot be seen to be.

Both Trump and Kim thought they had jobs for life and could do whatever they liked. The difference was that Kim was right.

4. LEADERSHIP

Communist, individualist, and most other leaderships serve individual and sectional interests. Nationalist leadership serves the nation. Idealistic leadership serves the ideals.

"(President) Trump already sounding calmer, less confrontational & more inclusive," his friend English broadcaster Piers Morgan tweeted shortly after the 2016 election. *"Augurs well. #USElection."*

It happened too rarely. Trump seldom acted like a president.

Trump was the first non-politician elected president since General Eisenhower answered what he felt was a call to national duty in 1952, but many people secure senior jobs in industries in which they have no experience. They learn. Others could have aided Trump, if he let them.

For most elected officials, the income and notoriety of office can become inadequate rewards, however adequate they once were. Most elected officials have some particular interest or range of interests driving them, more than implementing other people's agendas, at least when they reach the highest office to which they aspire. There was no higher office on earth than the American presidency.

With his wealth and fame already, Trump had more reason than most elected officials to focus on what he could achieve in office. There is no point in elected office without achieving something, whatever that something is.

In Trump's first two years in office, the Republican Party controlled the White House and both houses of Congress. Upon Trump's inauguration, it seemed the Republicans would deliver the promises they had made for years that Obama vetoed. Trump could honor everything he promised in the 2016 election.

When the Democrats controlled both houses of Congress through the first two years of the Obama presidency, Obama focused on healthcare. Trump never focused on anything for very long, befitting a man without nationalism, ideals, or conviction about anything, except himself.

The American presidency is an immense opportunity for leadership, within America and across the world, for presidents who want it. The presidency is a platform to try to bring people to their points of view.

In 1981, President Reagan entered the White House promising change. A Republican, he often conflicted with the seasoned House of Representatives speaker Tip O'Neill.

An old-style Democrat and more of a nationalist than Reagan, O'Neill considered Reagan the agent of the Republican rich. On a television talk show in 1981, he accused Reagan of having "no concern, no regard, no care for the little man of America."

In response, Reagan claimed that O'Neill used "sheer demagoguery" in politics. The next day, Reagan telephoned O'Neill to smooth the waters.

"Old buddy, that's politics," replied O'Neill. "After six o'clock, we can be friends, but before six, it's politics." O'Neill considered Reagan the most conservative man ever to enter the White House, but could not help but like the guy.

If Trump had the charm of Reagan, he would probably have been a better president. He would probably have been re-elected in 2020.

By 2016, Americans lauded those with whom they agreed and abused those with whom they did not. They sought to turn the latter into the former not with facts or reason, but with bullying and intimidation. Political correctness was abuse behind a mask of civility.

Trump was the same, but without the mask. In an era where few people sought to persuade their opponents to indecision or to bring the undecided to support them with argument or debate, neither did Trump.

Abuse is not strength or force in a personality. It is the weakness of not knowing what else to say.

Trump was at his charming and charismatic best among ordinary Americans, with whom he was comfortable. Trusting Trump to answer their frustrations developed over decades, they adored him and asked nothing of him, beyond his autograph.

In August 2020, Trump visited Lake Charles, Louisiana to inspect damage from Hurricane Laura. After taking questions from reporters, he signed autographs for other attendees. "Sell this on eBay tonight," he told one recipient. "You'll get ten thousand dollars." Making money was always on his mind.

With public figures, Trump could be publicly and pointlessly confrontational. He assailed people not giving him what he wanted, instead of getting what he wanted.

Trump's feuds never rested. In the middle of the night, perhaps with only a computer screen for company, Trump tweeted his abuse of people soundlessly asleep.

His criticisms did not normally confront the people concerned. People he could have telephoned or summoned to his office, including his appointees to government roles, Trump derided from a distance, for the world to see and hear. It affirmed the isolation in which he lived.

Assailing people might be good tactics for firing up far-away voters wanting someone to shake up Washington, emotionally appealing to people hating Washington, but it is the worst of all tactics for actually shaking up Washington. Abusing people antagonizes them, and is no way to bring audiences aboard. It might amuse audiences, but it also alienates audiences. If it shores up supporters there is nothing else to shore up that support.

When those individuals Trump abused were plainly not as strong as he was, Trump was a bully. Nationalists do not bully their compatriots. They should not bully anyone.

Trump's hatred was no more harmful than his opponents' hatred, but he had the opportunity to lead. Reciprocating their hatred denied him that opportunity.

People do not need to hate people because they disagree. They are more likely to persuade people and persuade their audience if they do not hate them. Charm gives a chance for logic to succeed.

That is especially the case with nationalism. At the core of nationalism is a common identity among compatriots, which keeps people from hating their compatriots however passionately they disagree. Common identities offer people a reason to make light of differences.

That can be hardest when their disagreement is over issues and actions harming their nation. Nationalists conflict with people damaging the nation, but might also consider what inspired their compatriots to become pitted against their people and countries.

The emotion that won in 2016 was a love for America. The emotion that lost in 2020 was Trump's hatred of people who defied him. Had Trump been re-elected, it would have compounded the confidence with which he berated anyone not lauding him.

Like other business leaders of his time, Trump was unsuited to democracy. Political deal-making is not business deal-making. Businessmen and women normally have choices of people with whom to deal. They can walk away.

Congress is a smaller pool. It is the only place for deals.

In the mid-term Congressional elections of 1994, Republican congressmen offered voters their Contract with America, comprising eight reforms the Republicans promised to enact and ten bills they would bring to a vote if Americans gave them control of Congress. Americans did, for the first time since 1953.

Republicans honored the Contract, although Congress failed to pass much of it. President Clinton vetoed or altered much of the rest through negotiation. American government never functioned better than it did with Newt Gingrich the Speaker of the House and Clinton in the White House, influencing and moderating each other.

Were Trump a nationalist, he would have seen at least some Democrats as his compatriots, especially moderate Democrats looking to re-engage with their lost supporters in 2017. He would have engaged with people with whom he disagreed, instead of berating them. He would have confined conflicts to policy, before making friends of an evening.

Successful people need allies. The bigger the task at hand, the more challenging and deeper the opposition, the more they need allies. No task is bigger, more challenging, and more opposed than trying to make America great again: a task for many people.

Leaders demonstrating their commitment to a cause, religion, or people attract people also committed to that cause, religion, or people. They attract allies in matters where they have common interests. By serving the nation, nationalist leaders attract nationalist allies. They then draw upon those allies.

There is no fault in being unable to succeed alone. There is fault in turning down assistance. There is greater fault in alienating assistance already in place.

Also born in New York but in 1941 to a Jewish family, Bernie Sanders became a congressman from Vermont in 1991 and a senator from Vermont in 2007. He was a socialist, although not the sanitized socialism of other rich people calling for equality and inclusion at other people's expense, without wanting anything to diminish their secure good lives.

Sanders' socialism was traditional socialism, which cared about poor Americans instead of everyone else: people who suffered instead of people claiming they suffered. He was willing to increase taxes upon himself if it increased taxes upon other rich people.

In 2007, Sanders opposed a comprehensive immigration reform bill. "At a time when the middle class is shrinking," he said, "the last thing we need is to bring, over a period of years, millions of people into this country who are prepared to lower wages for American workers."

Traditional Democrats recognized the harm that immigration did working-class people. They enforced America's borders.

Especially for being Jewish, Sanders might not have called himself an American nationalist, but for caring about America's poor, he was in effect a nationalist. Mixing nationalism with socialism did not mean National Socialism. It meant helping the poor of a person's country instead of the people of other countries.

Populism of the left and right are much alike. Populism is simply what is popular: what ordinary people want.

In 2015, with Sanders a candidate for the Democratic Party nomination, he could sound much like Trump. Sanders was no individualist, but before his election, Trump did not seem to be an individualist either. Presumably to earn votes in the Democratic primaries and caucuses of 2016, Sanders watered down his views of immigration.

Like Trump, Sanders led large rallies of enthusiastic supporters and people interested enough to be there. Like Trump, policy underpinned people's enthusiasm, but so did white people's need for a champion. Both men led movements wanting to change America, albeit in different directions.

A Co-operative Congressional Election Study from Harvard University reported that twelve percent of people voting for Sanders in the Democrat primaries of 2016 voted for Trump in the general election. Their cry for change proceeded from one change to another.

"To the degree that Mr. Trump is serious about pursuing policies that improve the lives of working families in this country," Sanders said in a statement after Trump's election in 2016, *"I and other progressives are prepared to work with him."* If Trump was a nationalist, he would have

taken up the offer, although differences remained. *"To the degree that he pursues racist, sexist, xenophobic and anti-environment policies, we will vigorously oppose him."*

Working upon common interests, leaders committed to a cause, religion, or people put differences aside. Those differences can be many. The common interest need only be one.

Again a candidate for the Democratic Party nomination in 2020, Sanders spoke more of being a Jew than he had spoken in 2016. Jewish by race but not by faith, it was Jewish nationalism, inviting support from fellow Jews, who remained so important a constituency among Democrats.

Like Trump, Sanders by 2020 had lost something of his populism: his traditional socialism. He promoted rights to homosexuality and so-called transgenderism as apparently he had for decades, but they were not what he was known for in 2015. They were causes for rich people looking for problems, rather than causes for poor people with problems in place.

By his failure to govern, Trump never ceased being the outsider that he rode to power being. He remained an outsider because he wanted to remain an outsider. There was less work to do.

When Trump hosted the television series *The Apprentice* for fourteen seasons from 2003, his catchphrase was "You're fired!" His presidency was much the same.

Trump appointed supportive newsman Steve Bannon his chief strategist, but in February 2017, Bannon appeared on the cover of *Time* magazine with the caption *"The Great Manipulator."* In April 2017, *The New York Times* newspaper reported that Trump was *"especially bothered"* with the cover.

Joshua Green's 2017 book *Devil's Bargain* credited Bannon with the intellectual force behind Trump's election. "That ... Steve Bannon taking credit for my election," complained Trump, according to a confidant quoted by *Buzz Feed News* in August 2017. Trump fired Bannon that month.

Nationalism wants outcomes for the people more than it dwells upon a president's sensitivities, but Trump's administration suffered an extraordinary turnover of personnel. He might have put too little thought in the people he appointed. He might have fired them for something other than performance.

Trump presided as American business leaders of the time presided, especially among corporations as big as Trump's corporations. Business leadership was dictatorship, by people empowered to do much as they liked, almost at will.

Firing people is not strength. It is the weakness of being unable to lead. The refuge of individualists, firing people is a weak substitute for managing or leading them.

Only the owners and sometimes bankers could fire business leaders. In 2020, voters fired Trump.

Among the many contrasts between Trump's presidency and other presidencies was how little profile his cabinet members built through their tenure, not only those whose tenures were so short. Men and women there for four years remained unseen and unheard.

"Are you worried that the State Department doesn't have enough Donald Trump nominees in there to push your vision through?" Laura Ingraham asked Trump on *The Ingraham Angle* in November 2017.

"…let me tell you," replied Trump. "The one that matters is me. I'm the only one that matters, because when it comes to it, that's what the policy is going to be. You've seen that, you've seen it strongly."

The spotlight rarely left Trump. He kept himself the star, as he insisted upon being, in a show slowly failing. He seemed to prefer to shine the brightest among stars with little shine, than share the shine with stars all shining brightly.

Nationalists do not need to be stars. They want their nations to shine. People committed to a cause, religion, or people want their cause, religion, or people the stars.

Nationalism recognizes the contributions that compatriots make. Trump could have collected the wisest minds in America and asked them how he could implement any of his promises and policies, different experts for different promises and policies. To do that, Trump would have needed to appoint people upon their credentials and willingness to implement those promises and policies, even if they previously objected.

His election having been founded upon nationalism, Trump would have needed to make nationalism a cornerstone of his administration. For all his rhetoric, he did not.

The cornerstone of Trump's one-man administration was people's subservience not to the American people, but to Trump. The only criterion by which a person seems to have lasted at

Trump's White House was his or her fealty to him.

Trump's limitless conviction in his capacity denied much of a role for other people. It is hard enough to be an expert about anything, let alone one about everything. Whether it was bravado or he was sincere, Trump declared himself expert in pretty well everything.

Wise men and women recognize their ignorance. Good leaders appoint talented people and give them clear objectives. Leaders might suggest actions, but they empower people to determine how best to achieve those objectives. Wanting a plurality of opinion from which the best outcomes unfold, meetings can be brief, if attendees have their say, make clear decisions, and leave knowing what to do. Leaders need only intervene when necessary or desirable.

Nationalists delegate, to their compatriots. Trump did not. He gave instructions. He involved himself in matters in which he had no expertise.

Nor did he decide. Too few decisions were made.

He was no dictator, however much he wished he was. He was no fascist, as critics feared he would be. He was barely even president.

Leaders need to know their limitations, to recognize their capacity for error. They need people to teach them, or correct them.

Thus leaders need the confidence to appoint people willing to advise them they are wrong. Leaders need not take that advice, but they must be willing to hear it.

Trump surrounded himself with people unwilling to set boundaries to his impulses. It denied him reason to question his actions, even as his re-election campaign barreled towards defeat. It denied him information to save him.

People need to hear bad news, however difficult it is. Only then can they deal with it.

Trump did not respond to bad news. He responded to the person expressing it. He fired him.

In October 2019, former White House chief of staff John Kelly told the *Washington Examiner* magazine that he warned Trump not to replace him with someone who would accede to Trump's dictate. "I said whatever you do, don't hire a 'yes man,' someone who won't tell you the truth. Don't do that, because if you do, I believe you will be impeached."

Kelly was right. Trump's telephone call with Ukrainian president Volodymyr Zelensky in July 2019 led to the House of Representatives impeaching Trump on two charges in December 2019.

More interesting than any illegality about Trump's words and actions, was that Trump took such an interest in pressing a foreign leader to investigate allegations against Democrat presidential candidate Joe Biden's son Hunter Biden. Instead of making America great again, Trump worried about his political opponents' every move. Trump waged personal battles instead of national battles.

Acquitted by the Senate in February 2020, a normal president might have felt chastened for having been impeached. If anything, Trump appeared even more emboldened to do whatever he wanted to do. It invited him to be impeached again, in January 2021.

5. LOYALTY

Leaders committed to a cause, religion, or people demand loyalty to that cause, religion, or people. If nationalists demand loyalty, it is loyalty to the nation. Nationalism is about the nation: the people.

By their nationalism or other commitment to their cause, religion, or people, leaders might attract the personal loyalty of fellow devotees. Nationalist loyalty endures because nationalism endures. Other loyalties endure because the cause, religion, or people endure. All the leader needs to do is maintain his or her nationalism or other commitment.

Mutual loyalty is in both people's interests. Nationalism is in all compatriots' interests.

From the moment in 2015 that Trump announced his candidacy for the Republican Party nomination for president, he defied political norms of his era. He talked about issues that the Republican Party preferred only to hint about, without dealing with.

Nevertheless, the Republican National Committee conducted its primaries and caucuses fairly. The result appeared to be a greater engagement from ordinary Republicans with the eventual candidate, Trump, than Democrats enjoyed, after the Democrat National Committee favored Hillary Clinton over Bernie Sanders.

Republicans voted for Trump because he was a Republican. Generally, Republicans that did not support Trump did not draw attention to their lack of support. During his presidency, Republican congressmen and women voted with Trump because he too was a Republican.

People are not disloyal for thinking independently, rationally considering issues on their merits, and calmly disagreeing with someone. In a May 2020 television commercial for his primary campaign, Nebraska senator Ben Sasse told voters he sometimes agreed and sometimes disagreed with Trump. *"None of my disagreements are personal,"* tweeted Sasse in August 2020, after Trump *"moved our conversation from private to public."*

In Trump's first trial before the Senate, early in 2020, Sasse voted against the calling of witnesses in pursuit of evidence one way or the other as to Trump's guilt, implicitly not seeing even the first step towards a conviction having been reached. Sasse voted to acquit him.

Renowned for not being intimated by anyone, Maine senator Susan Collins voted to confirm Trump's nomination of Justice Brett Kavanaugh to the Supreme Court in 2018, relying on the evidence before her and applying reason carefully laid out in her speech before the Senate. At Trump's first trial before the Senate, Collins was one of only two Republicans voting to call witnesses. When witnesses were not called, Collins voted on the evidence before her to acquit him.

At Trump's second trial before the Senate, in February 2021 with his presidency already over, Sasse and Collins joined five other Republicans and every Democrat in finding Trump guilty of having incited an insurrection at the Capitol Building in January 2021. In Sasse and Collins' view at least, reason and the evidence would have required it.

Individualists demand personal loyalty. They do not reciprocate it.

Trump did not reciprocate the loyalty he received from Republicans. Especially in his determination to retain power at the end of his presidency, he assailed Republicans not deferring to his demands. The Republican Party delivered Trump the presidency in 2016, but he proved willing to punish the Party for being unable to overcome his failings in office and deliver him re-election in 2020.

In 2015, the Fox television network was close to the Republican Party establishment, so initially no friend to Trump's rogue candidacy. When Trump became assured of the Republican Party nomination in 2016, Fox became supportive.

Having confined himself to people who roared their approval at his rallies and did not defy him in private, Trump seemed to develop through his presidency a skewed impression of the world and his place in it, as rich and powerful people often do. Poor opinion polling made no sense to him, except as his opponents lying. Trump expected as much from other broadcast networks, but not from Fox. *Fox News* reported opinion polling that other networks reported.

What could have been a message for Trump that something

about his presidency was failing became a reason for him to turn against Fox. "*.@FoxNews just doesn't get what's happening!*" Trump tweeted in April 2020. "*They are being fed Democrat talking points, and they play them without hesitation or research. They forgot that Fake News @CNN & MSDNC wouldn't let @FoxNews participate, even a little bit, in the poor ratings Democrat Debates...*"

Fox remained friendlier to Trump than other media, but it was less than the pandering that Trump demanded: without question or compromise, whatever the facts. Trump's assaulting of Fox worsened after *Fox News* called Arizona for Joe Biden on the night of the 2020 election. Most things about Trump worsened after his election loss.

"*.@FoxNews daytime ratings have completely collapsed,*" Trump tweeted in November 2020. "*Weekend daytime even WORSE. Very sad to watch this happen, but they forgot what made them successful, what got them there. They forgot the Golden Goose. The biggest difference between the 2016 Election, and 2020, was @FoxNews!*"

The biggest difference between the 2016 election and 2020 was not Fox News. It was Trump's four years in office.

The only people that Trump treated worse than his opponents were his supporters, falling short of his every command, not acceding to his every whim. While demanding unwavering loyalty from others, Trump was manifestly disloyal.

In 2016, in spite of his long public service, Alabama senator Jeff Sessions had not succumbed to Washington. A Southern gentleman, as few men still were, he maintained honor while it became increasingly rare in America and even rarer in Washington. For many years, he had been a consistent voice against immigration and the harm it did Americans, especially the poor, as few congressmen were. He was the most reliable force for nationalism in a city that had grown increasingly estranged from America and Americans.

Addressing a Trump rally in Madison, Alabama in February 2016, Sessions became the first sitting senator to endorse Trump's candidacy. For many observers, it legitimized Trump's candidacy.

In return, after his election, Trump nominated Sessions to be attorney general. In 2017, lawyers at the Department of Justice advised Sessions to recuse himself from overseeing Special Counsel Robert Mueller's investigation into alleged Russian collusion with Trump's 2016 campaign, after allegations that Sessions met the

Russian ambassador during the campaign. Sessions had forgotten those encounters.

Were Sessions not to recuse himself, then any finding from the investigation that there had been no collusion would be tainted. It was thus in Trump's interest that Sessions recuse himself.

Trump did not care. He did not accede to the lawyers' advice. He did not worry about the impression cast by Sessions overseeing Mueller's investigation.

"Sessions should have never recused himself," Trump told *The New York Times* newspaper in July 2017, "and if he was going to recuse himself, he should have told me before he took the job and I would have picked somebody else."

Trump expected even his most loyal supporters to abandon all principle in submission to him. After months of media speculation, Trump sought and obtained Sessions' resignation in November 2018.

Sessions was among the many to fall foul of Trump, but Trump's treatment of Sessions was particularly cruel. Not content with driving Sessions from office, Trump continued tweeting abuse.

When Sessions sought to return to the Alabama Senate seat from which he retired to serve as Trump's attorney general, Trump campaigned against him. "*3 years ago*," Trump tweeted in May 2020, "*after Jeff Sessions recused himself, the Fraudulent Mueller Scam began. Alabama, do not trust Jeff Sessions. He let our Country down.*"

"*Look*," tweeted Sessions in reply, "*I know your anger, but recusal was required by law. I did my duty & you're damn fortunate I did. It protected the rule of law & resulted in your exoneration.*" Trump still did not care.

Sessions had long been popular among the people who voted Trump into office, but Trump was the president. Sessions lost.

Through it all, Sessions maintained his support of Trump. He never ceased being an honorable man, even when those around him were not. That only amplified Trump's dishonor.

For Trump to have no loyalty to a nationalist like Sessions was to prove Trump not to be a nationalist. Trump's interest was self-interest, but not a practical, rational self-interest. It was a tiny, vindictive self-interest, which derived more pleasures from feelings inside his head than from holding what could have been the most powerful office on earth.

People who condemned Trump for criticizing immigration had

long condemned Sessions for the same reason. They might not have noticed any impact that Trump's treatment of Sessions had upon people supporting both men, risking Trump's Oval Office to deny Sessions his old Senate seat again.

Trump's quarrels left Trump alone when the time came that he needed people's support. Might Trump have won in 2020 had he not treated Sessions as he did, but with Sessions campaigning for him? Among the tragedies of the Trump presidency was that its most enduring legacies should include removing Sessions from the Senate.

William Barr served as attorney general to President George H W Bush from 1991 to 1993. In 2019, Trump again appointed him attorney general.

Whatever Barr and Sessions had in common, their differences were more pronounced. Both men were tough, but burly Bill Barr was more obviously tougher. The criticisms of Sessions that he was too polite did not apply to Barr. Most importantly, Barr understood that the role of every person in the Trump administration was to do as Trump directed. Barr became a rare Cabinet member with a public profile.

As well as the most senior law officer in America, Barr appeared for the world to behave like Trump's personal attorney, ensuring Barr's survival and authority in the role. He pursued matters of no great import, except to Trump.

The Department of Justice sued Stephanie Winston Wolkoff for profits from her revelatory book *Melania and Me*, published in September 2020. They had been friends for almost two decades.

"So now Bill Barr is not just DONALD Trump's lawyer / fixer-but he is also MELANIA Trump's lawyer?" tweeted legal analyst Glenn Kirschner in October 2020.

Early in February 2021, a few weeks after President Biden took office, the Department of Justice withdrew its case against Wolkoff. "The Department evaluated the case," said a Department official, "and concluded that dismissal without prejudice was in the best interests of the United States based on the facts and the law."

Ultimately, Barr fell afoul of Trump for the same reason that Sessions did. The two attorneys general told the truth and complied with the law, but Trump's demand for fealty allowed no limits in others that Trump did not feel in himself, and Trump suffered few limits.

Trump's fixation with his political foes reached to his foes from the past. If Trump had a third interest after tweeting and golf, it was Hillary Clinton's mail: her use of a private electronic mail server for official communications during her tenure as Secretary of State, which ended in February 2013, and her deletion of that mail. In July 2016, the Federal Bureau of Investigation found her actions to have been careless but lacking criminal intent. Talk of her actions in 2016 was political campaigning, but she ceased to be a candidate with the 2016 election.

In 2020, Barr's Department of Justice found no evidence of criminal wrongdoing by Clinton. "To be honest," Trump told *Fox Business* in October 2020, "Bill Barr is going to go down as either the greatest attorney general in the history of the country or he's going to go down as, you know, a very sad situation... He's got all the information he needs. They want to get more, more, more. They keep getting more. I said, 'you don't need any more'."

The problems with demanding personal loyalty are many. People pretend to be loyal. They abandon one loyalty for a better offer.

Self-serving individualists attract sycophants. They attract people no less self-serving than they are.

When it mattered, Barr acted against Trump's interests. That might have been because it was in Barr's interests, especially near the end of Trump's presidency. That might have been to ensure that it would be the end of Trump's presidency, if Barr remained at heart a Bush Republican. Barr kept secret before the 2020 election a Department of Justice investigation into Democrat nominee Joe Biden's son Hunter.

Barr's secrecy was a pointed contrast to Federal Bureau of Investigation director James Comey in October 2016, informing Congress of a renewed investigation into Hillary Clinton's electronic mail. "*Assuming,*" wrote Comey in his 2018 book *A Higher Loyalty*, "*as nearly everyone did, that Hillary Clinton would be elected president of the United States in less than two weeks, what would happen to the FBI, the justice department or her own presidency if it later was revealed, after the fact, that she still was the subject of an FBI investigation?*"

In her 2017 book *What Happened*, Hillary Clinton wrote: "*If not for the dramatic intervention of the FBI director in the final days we would have won the White House.*"

Barr could well have presumed a similar impact upon Biden's

campaign in 2020, if Barr revealed the investigation into Hunter Biden before the election. Laws and honor mandate different responses to different situations, but might Sessions if he was still attorney general in 2020 have felt honor bound to reveal to Congress and so voters the investigation into Biden's son before the election, as Comey felt in respect of the Clinton investigation four years earlier? Might Trump have been re-elected in 2020 with Sessions still his attorney general?

Individualism does not benefit the individualists as much as they presume it does. More often than not, it harms them.

Even by Trump's tireless tweeting, he tweeted a lot about Barr in December 2020. *"A big disappointment!"* Trump tweeted, sharing a tweet that called for Barr to be fired.

"IF Biden gets in," began another tweet, *"nothing will happen to Hunter or Joe. Barr will do nothing, and the new group of partisan killers coming in will quickly kill it all."*

"Why didn't Bill Barr reveal the truth to the public, before the Election, about Hunter Biden," Trump tweeted. *"Joe was lying on the debate stage that nothing was wrong, or going on – Press confirmed. Big disadvantage for Republicans at the polls!"*

At the start of December 2020, Barr reported the results of the Department of Justice investigations into Trump's claims of fraud in the 2020 election. "To date," said Barr, "we have not seen fraud on a scale that could have effected a different outcome in the election."

"I guess he's the next one to be fired," remarked Senate Democrat leader Chuck Schumer.

The last months of any presidency are normally lame, but Trump's presidency continued the chaos. Barr resigned, effective before Christmas.

People giving no loyalty receive no loyalty. Trump, the individualist, became more alone.

6. FAMILIES

In his 1992 presidential campaign, Bill Clinton said of him and his wife Hillary that, if Americans elected him president, they would "get two for the price of one." After his election, Hillary established an office in the West Wing of the White House. She developed and promoted the Clinton healthcare plan, which Congress declined to adopt in 1994.

Amidst nationalism, families are the center of connectedness between people. Relatives identifying in their common family, sharing their family interest, are the cores of compatriots and nations doing the same. Families and nations express themselves through each individual among them.

That Trump's name dominated the names of his family businesses and properties could have expressed his family. It could have expressed him.

Amidst individualism, families become another means of individuals pursuing their individual self-interests. Individuals express themselves through their relatives, primarily their children, as if those relatives were simply extensions of them. Those relatives might not oblige.

Trump's niece Mary Trump campaigned against him with her July 2020 book *Too Much and Never Enough*, subtitled *How My Family Created the World's Most Dangerous Man*. That might have been her revenge for Trump's treatment of her and her father. It might have been her politics, proudly placed ahead of racial and other familial loyalty. Her homosexuality might have expressed hostility to her family. Her lesbianism might have reflected hostility to men. They might all have been her reactions to her uncle Donald. Individualism breaks down families.

Sometimes, bad people appear in good families. Less often, good people appear in bad families. People behave differently in different situations, and with different people.

Trump made much of his children. While he was president, his sons Eric and Donald, Junior managed the Trump businesses.

He treated the presidency like another family business. Only he and his family seemed to hold much authority.

Was Donald, Junior's girlfriend Kimberly Guilfoyle the best person to lead Trump's finance team in 2020? In November 2020, *Politico* reported that she frequently joked about her sex life and at one fundraiser offered a lap dance to the most generous donor.

Presidents should consult their families. They should not defer to them, especially in-laws.

In Trump's West Wing, his elder daughter Ivanka maintained an office. She and her husband Jared Kushner could attend any meeting they wanted to attend, join lunches with foreign leaders, and walk into Trump's Oval Office at any time.

A fellow New York property developer, Kushner earned mentions through the 2016 election campaign because he was Jewish, an observant Orthodox Jew, proving that Trump was not racist or anti-Semitic. Trump's grandchildren included Kushner's three Jewish children.

After Trump's election, federal authorities recommended that Kushner not get security clearance because he provided false information to them about his contacts with foreigners. Trump ordered that Kushner receive clearance.

Michael Wolff's 2018 book *Fire and Fury* referred to Trump, before his inauguration, considering appointing Kushner his chief of staff. Supporter Ann Coulter took Trump aside. "Nobody is apparently telling you this," she told Trump, "but you can't. You just can't hire your children." Trump appointed Kushner a senior adviser.

In April 2017, Coulter explained to Mark Mardell of BBC Radio 4 that her view was nothing personal to Kushner. It was a matter of principle, applicable to all presidents, their children, and their children-in-law. Mardell quoted an unnamed source that Kushner reflected "the views of his New York friends, who hate Trump."

"He has been the link from the Trump campaign to Wall Street," Lizzie Widdicombe, an editor of *The New Yorker* magazine's 'Talk of the town' told Mardell, "and he has emerged as a powerbroker."

Kushner did not publicly flaunt any influence over Trump. He maintained a Twitter account, but did not tweet.

In spite of Senator John McCain having not wanted Trump at his funeral in September 2018, Kushner and Ivanka Trump attended. McCain's widow said later that the McCain family had not invited them.

While Ivanka Trump and other Trump children spoke at the 2020 Republican Party convention, Kushner did not. That might have been because he was above the convention, pulling strings.

Did Kushner convince Trump to keep Jeff Sessions from the Senate in 2020 when Sessions tried to return to elected office, thinking that Sessions was a threat to Kushner's second-term agenda? If Kushner and Trump were so certain there would be a second term says much about the reasons there was not. If Kushner felt Sessions threatened that second-term agenda, then it might be better that the agenda was never implemented.

The electorate gets things right. Speaking to students at the University of Texas, Austin in November 2020, Ann Coulter said that Trump "deserved to lose" the 2020 election. She blamed it on Trump abandoning his 2016 agenda on the advice of "wonder boy" Kushner.

Living as Kushner lived among people hating Trump, ignorant of the people who voted for Trump in 2016, Kushner might have thought he was helping his father-in-law be re-elected. Alternatively, he might have preferred one presidency on his terms than none. Kushner might have led Trump more than Trump led anyone.

Trump deserved to win the 2016 election for the promises he made. He deserved to lose the 2020 election for the promises he failed to keep.

The American tragedy was not that Trump lost the 2020 election. It was that he deserved to lose.

The presidency that promised so much delivered much less. Had he implemented his promises in 2016, especially around trade and immigration, drawing upon the people who supported him in 2016, then he could have helped make America great again.

Did Trump ever intend to make America great again, or did he just like saying it and hearing the applause? Did he ever intend anything he promised?

Was Trump serious about his trade war with China? Did he do all that he could do to revive American manufacturing?

Why did he not build the wall along the Mexican border? Why did he not deport illegal immigrants? Did agricultural and other business interests persuade him that they needed labor cheaper than Americans' entitlements?

Why did Trump not cut immigration? Did the bankers to his business interests threaten their funding? Did big business persuade Congress and Trump to leave the law as it was? In an interview with *The Daily Caller* in December 2018, Ann Coulter surmised that so "Ivanka and Jared can make money ... seems to be the main point of the presidency at this point."

In Trump's administration, Kushner's responsibilities included peace in the Middle East. For decades, American presidential candidates had promised, if they became president, to move America's embassy in Israel to Jerusalem, recognizing Jerusalem as the Israeli capital. Trump was the first president to honor that promise.

Trump announced the move in December 2017. The Jerusalem embassy opened in May 2018.

It is unlikely that any person voting for Trump in the 2016 election did so because of that promise. It was not an issue for a family in rural Kentucky trying to pay the rent.

Nevertheless, that family in rural Kentucky might have supported Trump's decision on moral grounds, if it ever thought about it. Every country on earth bar one could choose its capital city, with other countries respecting that choice and locating their embassies or high commissions there. They might have consular offices and high commissions in other cities and they might not have any representation in a country, but they never challenged a county's right to choose its capital, except when that country was Israel.

Jerusalem was, in effect, the Jewish capital in ancient times. It was the site of Solomon's Temple and then the Second Temple, destroyed in AD 70. In 1980, Israel declared Jerusalem its capital.

Jewish nationalism prospered through the Trump presidency. Surveys by the Pew Research Center in Washington in the spring of 2019 reported that Israel was the only country in which a majority of people expressed net approval of Trump's principal foreign policies. America offered the second-highest net approval, but still a minority.

American Jews, like other racial minorities, increased their vote for Trump from 2016 to 2020. The Associated Press' Vote Cast survey of 2020 suggested that increase was approximately five percent.

Within that figure, there might have been different increases. In November 2020, Nishma Research in Connecticut noted past studies showing that American Jews were overwhelmingly Democrat, but a huge majority of Haredi ultra-Orthodox American Jews were Republican and Modern Orthodox Jews were more evenly split between Democrats and Republicans. The more religious Jews were, the more they voted Republican.

If his American critics gave Trump credit for anything, it was some small credit for the peace treaties signed between Israel and some Arab states in 2020 known as the Abraham Accords, although his critics never gave Trump as much credit as he gave himself. Trump might not have been making America great again, but he was making Israel safe.

When first reports appeared in December 2020 of any interest from the White House in anything but Trump's claims of electoral fraud in the 2020 election, it was of Trump trying to do more not for America, but for the Middle East. He was continuing to work for peace treaties between Israel and Arab states.

That might have been Kushner's achievement, after he applied the authority his father-in-law gave him to trip around the Middle East. In December 2020, Israeli prime minister Benjamin Netanyahu presented Kushner with a certificate of appreciation for "his historic contribution to the Abraham Accords." Such a certificate might have seemed little more than a gold star on the back of Kushner's hand, but that an Israeli prime minister should give an American presidential senior adviser anything was telling.

While Trump's foreign policy mantra was America First, the promises he kept and accomplishments he made were more in the nature of Israel First. It was nationalism, but Jewish nationalism, respecting Arab tribalism.

One of Trump's final actions as president was ordering that the United States Central Command include Israel as the twenty-first country within its Area of Responsibility. Advocates for Israel believed that it aided strategic co-operation against Iran.

Trump maintained the tradition of American presidents pardoning their friends, donors, and other criminals of interest in the last months of their presidency. This being the Trump presidency, he also reportedly contemplated pre-emptively pardoning himself and his children, although none of them had been charged with a crime.

Among the criminals Trump pardoned in December 2020 was Jared Kushner's father, Charles Kushner. In 2004, Charles Kushner pleaded guilty to eighteen crimes, including tax evasion, making illegal contributions to political campaigns, and witness tampering.

With his sister and brother-in-law co-operating with federal authorities in their investigations of him, Charles Kushner paid ten thousand dollars to a prostitute to lure his brother-in-law to a hotel room and seduce him. Kushner recorded the seduction and gave the recording to his sister during her son's engagement party.

The prosecutor was Chris Christie, who later became New Jersey governor. In January 2019, Christie told the *Firing Line* television program that Charles Kushner committed "one of the most loathsome, disgusting crimes that I prosecuted when I was U.S. attorney." Kushner served fourteen months in jail.

In 2016, Christie worked on the transition into the Trump presidency. "*I did everything I could to make sure my friend Donald reached the White House fully prepared to serve,*" Christie wrote in his 2019 memoir *Let Me Finish.* "*But a handful of selfish individuals sidetracked our very best efforts. They set loose toxic forces that have made Trump's presidency far less effective than it would otherwise have been.*"

Christie wrote of Steve Bannon informing him that Jared Kushner was "taking an ax to your head with the boss ever since I got here." The boss was Trump. "It's been constant. He never stops. Ancient bitterness, I guess." Kushner succeeded in expelling Christie from Trump's inner circle, "*still apparently seething over events that had occurred a decade ago.*"

Might the chaotic Trump presidency have begun better had Trump utilized Christie's work on his transition to power? Christie's governorship of New Jersey had controversy, but his successes in his first term led to him being comfortably re-elected to a second term. He had the brashness that could have suited Trump and he understood the workings of government.

Had Trump's appointments been based upon merit, then Christie was a candidate worthy of consideration. Christie was reportedly considered for the attorney general role before it went to William Barr. In December 2018, after a meeting with Trump, Christie said he did not want to be Trump's chief of staff.

If loyalty to Trump had been the only qualification for office, then Christie's support of Trump after ending his presidential campaign in February 2016 would have assured him of office, but loyalty to Trump was not enough. Christie never was appointed to a role in the Trump administration.

Trump's presidency might not have been the presidency of Israel First. It might have been the presidency of Kushner First.

Might Trump have been a better president and re-elected in 2020 had Ivanka Trump married someone else? In her 2017 book *Raising Trump*, Trump's first wife Ivana Trump wrote that Trump wanted their daughter Ivanka to become involved with footballer Tom Brady, "*But Ivanka wasn't into it.*"

"Jared and I are very similar in that we're very ambitious," Ivanka Trump told *New York* magazine in July 2009, when they announced their engagement. She was converting to Judaism.

According to the New York City Board of Elections, Ivanka Trump did not change her party affiliation from Democrat to Republican until October 2018. "I am a proud Trump Republican," she told *The New York Times* newspaper in March 2020.

Ivanka Trump's choice of husband might prove to have been the single most destructive matrimonial decision in American history, but who would not take an opportunity to influence, even direct, an American president? If Trump accommodated Kushner's ambition, making Kushner a Rasputin-like figure in the White House shadows with a seeming hypnotic influence on Trump, then that was not Kushner's fault.

It was Trump's fault. The decisions were his. Trump was the president.

7. INTEGRITY

"The supreme quality for leadership is unquestionably integrity," said President Eisenhower, according to John Cheley's 1958 book *Stories for Talks with Boys and Girls*. "Without it, no real success is possible, no matter whether it is on a section gang, a football field, in an army, or in an office."

When America was great, Americans had integrity. They expected it in each other. They taught it to their children.

Whatever else might be said of American presidents since Eisenhower, the only president in whom there still appears a widespread confidence in his integrity was Carter. That did not make Carter widely considered a successful president and he failed to be re-elected in 1980, although he might have become the most successful former president.

The connectedness of nationalism and a common identity commands integrity between compatriots. In their personal and familial self-interests, nationalists can fall short of their ideals and often do, but they do so for a reason and feel ashamed for it.

With individualism, Americans lost their internal sanction: their conscience. Individualists act wantonly, unless they have interests in being seen to have integrity. Integrity became a matter of what people are seen to be, rather than what they are. Other individualists, or people from other nations, are only interested in their integrity to the extent it affects them.

Integrity is moral strength. Most obviously, it includes honesty.

Americans took to lying whenever telling the truth was difficult or when lies suited them more. President Nixon's great wrong, for which his Republican Party as well as Democrats required him to resign, was lying to the American people. In 1974, America retained enough nationalism to make lying untenable, at least in a president. Previous presidents had not been caught lying, while in office.

Intelligent people do not normally lie about something in respect of which their lie will be revealed. In 1972, a break-in at the

Democratic National Committee headquarters in the Watergate complex of office buildings in Washington seemed relatively insignificant. Revealing Nixon's lies about his knowledge of the break-in required two years of persistent investigation by reporters Bob Woodward and Carl Bernstein, as well as good fortune.

Whether President Reagan lied when he said he did not authorize the trading of arms to Iran for the release of American hostages held in Lebanon by Iranian-linked Hezbollah, and other aspects of the Iran–Contra scandal in the 1980s, remained known only to him and, perhaps, people close to him. The American public held views, but did not know.

There was often doubt as to whether a president lied. For the most part, voters supporting a president in respect of an issue did not believe he lied. People opposed to the president believed he lied. America was becoming increasingly less concerned with integrity generally.

In 1998, President Clinton lied about his relationship with pretty young intern Monica Lewinsky. He acknowledged the fault that lying still was by making torturous legalistic gymnastics that he had not lied: that his actions with Lewinsky were not sexual relations. By 1998, Democrats were less concerned with presidents lying than they had been when Nixon and allegedly Reagan lied.

Republicans cared that Clinton lied under oath. Voters cared less.

A man should not commit adultery or anything like it, but if he does commit it, then he should lie about it. Honesty would selfishly degrade his wife, family, and the precious institute of marriage. President Kennedy's infidelity remained hidden from general knowledge until after his death.

If President George W Bush and British prime minister Tony Blair believed that Iraq had weapons of mass destruction in 2003, their lie was about the evidence of those weapons. If America and Britain's invasion of Iraq that year uncovered those weapons, then their lying about the evidence should never have been revealed, although they might not have cared about being caught having lied. They might simply have wanted to invade Iraq.

Whether President Obama lied when he said that "if you like your healthcare plan, you can keep it" under his Affordable Health Care Act was less important to all sides than the Act itself. If his lie helped Obama Care become law, then its supporters probably saw any lie as worthwhile.

That was the environment in which Trump came to office. When a country decides to lie and accept lies, limits can be hard to impose.

In 2016, Trump was elected with a romantic view of business integrity, from the time of Eisenhower when America was great: a time of nationalism. Businessmen changed as Americans changed.

"He'll exaggerate for the purpose of making a sale," architect Der Scutt, who designed Trump Tower in New York, euphemistically said of Trump in 1976. Trump exaggerated in his business career. He continued exaggerating in his political career, making a sale.

Hyperbole is not a lie. It is mere puffery.

Trump was smart enough to know the falsehoods he made, if he considered them. Only he knew whether he was sincere or he knew he was lying.

Some people believe what they say. Others believe what they hear. Most do both, of what they say or hear often enough.

It was the era of postmodernism, in which truth and lies were interchangeable and something was true because people said it was true, in spite of the evidence. Trump's untruths were like other opinion leaders saying, for example, that interracial immigration enriched America, Islam was the religion of peace, homosexuals were born homosexual, or the so-called trans-women were women. Trump's purposes were no less political and commercial than were other lying people's purposes.

With political correctness consuming public figures and increasingly everyone else, lies abounded. Facts went unmentioned.

Pivotal to Trump's appeal for many people was his rejection of political correctness. Trump's criticisms of immigration were self-evident to people accustomed to being unable to say so, beyond their closest friends and confidants. Far from the loud voices of politicians and other public figures, ordinary Americans knew that terrorists were overwhelmingly Muslim.

Rejecting political correctness gave Trump authenticity. It obscured his lies about other matters.

Unlike his predecessors, Trump made lies that were blatant and easily proven to be lies. He lied about unimportant matters.

President-elect Trump told *The New York Times* newspaper that his inauguration in January 2017 would draw an "unbelievable, perhaps record-setting turnout." It was a pointless boast by a man already elected, which invited comparisons with President Obama's record-setting crowd eight years earlier.

"President Trump's Inauguration Crowd Doesn't Look like Barack Obama's Did in 2009," mocked *Time* magazine. Photographs of the two events showed the crowd for Trump's inauguration to be much smaller, but still average among inauguration crowds.

That set off a White House and media fixation with something of no importance, except that Trump made it important. Trump was still selling himself.

A day after his inauguration, Trump sent White House press secretary Sean Spicer out to challenge the media reports. "This was the largest audience to ever witness an inauguration – period – both in person and around the globe," said Spicer of Trump's inauguration, reading from a prepared statement. Analysis after analysis confirmed that it was not.

Trump was a prolific liar in an era of prolific liars. The difference was in the lies that he told and that he could be the only person saying his.

Trump's lies served only to harm him. They diminished his credibility among people who neither loved him nor loathed him, for nothing in return. By lying so frequently, Trump diminished the prospects of people believing him when he told the truth, as often he did.

Economic protection protects not only working people. It protects everyone.

Tariffs and other economic protection work outside the West. They worked in America too, before America dismantled them.

American manufacturing having become dependent upon foreign steel and other materials, reinstating tariffs needed to be careful, among a raft of measures to protect American industry. Without other measures, President George W Bush's tariffs on steel imports in 2002 might or might not have aided American jobs, before the World Trade Organization found them in breach of American trade commitments. They were abolished in 2003.

As he promised before his election, Trump improved upon the North American Free Trade Agreement. Opinion was mixed as to whether he could have improved it more.

Along with honesty, integrity means honoring one's promises. That is not quite the same as honesty. A promise made with the intention to honor it is not a lie. The lack of integrity is in later not honoring that promise.

Trump promised to revive American manufacturing through correcting trade, tax, and regulatory imbalances. To that end, Trump repealed many of the Obama administration policies strangling business in pursuit of consumer-related, environmental, and climate objectives.

Nationalists care deeply for the environment. They are simply not willing to sacrifice their compatriots' jobs, or their jobs, pointlessly. They are not willing to dismantle Western Civilization.

Pipelines are the safest, cleanest, and most efficient means of transporting oil, but in 2015, President Obama delayed construction of the Phase IV extension of the Keystone XL Pipeline due to environmentalists' hostility to oil and other carbon-based fossil fuels. In 2017, President Trump permitted completion of the pipeline. On his first day in office, President Biden signed an executive order revoking that permission.

Trump essentially honored his promises concerning carbon, including withdrawing America from the Paris Agreement of 2016. President Biden promptly returned her to the Paris Agreement.

Biden could repeal much of what Trump did in office with little real effect. He began doing so on his first day in office. Trump's much-vaunted repeals will last only until another president reinstates them. So might Biden's.

Trump promised much before he was elected and promised much afterwards, but his promises were not really promises. They were making a sale.

Instead of feeling any moral or political obligation to honor his promises, Trump seems to have honored particular promises because he happened to want to take those particular actions anyway. Instead of admitting his failure to fulfil other promises, he lied.

Fake news was a phrase of long standing, which Hillary Clinton used in a speech in December 2016. Trump began using it publicly in January 2017.

It would become Trump's stock reply to news reports he did not like. *"Wow,"* Trump tweeted in October 2017, *"so many Fake News stories today. No matter what I do or say, they will not write or speak truth. The Fake News Media is out of control!"*

Liars presume that others lie too. In an era when something was true for being said to be true, something else was fake for being said to be fake. The answer to people saying bad news was to stop them saying it, as if that made the news no longer true. Facts were immaterial.

Trump did not disprove allegations made against him. He did not take adverse news as problems he needed to redress, even if the only problem was his messaging. Without thought of the impact upon Americans of the matters reported, Trump simply labelled bad news as fake news.

His opponents were much the same, labelling truths that Trump told as bigotry or one phobia or another. Nobody still held a consistent devotion to the truth: to reality.

Among the thousands of journalists in information-loaded America by 2020, none enjoyed a reputation above that of Bob Woodward. For Woodward's 2020 book *Rage*, Trump granted Woodward eighteen interviews, in which Trump admitted lying to America.

In early February 2020, Trump was publicly comparing the Wuhan virus to a strain of influenza, which in time would disappear. At the same time, he told Woodward that the virus was deadlier than normal influenza. In March 2020, Trump told Woodward that he lied to avoid panic among the people and to save the American government's purchasing of gloves, masks, and other protective equipment from price gouging.

Anybody trying to keep a secret does not reveal it to a journalist, especially a journalist writing a book. Even anonymous, confidential, and clandestine briefings of journalists impart information.

In September 2020, after publication of Woodward's book, Trump defended his lies. "We had to show calm," he told journalists. "The last thing you can show is panic, excitement, or fear. We have to show leadership and leadership is confidence."

Trump's presidency exuded confidence. It was rarely calm.

Finding a theme through it all is difficult, but it seemed that Trump was comfortable being seen to lie. Knowing that America had become comfortable with lies, Trump feared being seen as incompetent or wrong. All that mattered was making a sale.

Of all the lies Trump could have told through his life, pretending to care for Americans through the pandemic would have been a good one. Trump did not need to be a nationalist if he pretended to be a nationalist, which might have been all he ever did. Being seen as compassionate seems not to have occurred to him.

With nationalist leadership comes responsibility to serve the nation, even if it encounters opposition. Nationalist leadership is not just an opportunity to tell truths that are otherwise not said. It is an obligation to tell them.

Individualist leadership feels no responsibility because individualism feels no responsibility. Trump's nationalism was fake.

Trump was not a good liar. Good liars are not known for being liars.

As his presidency concluded, it was hard to think of any lie Trump made that most people believed. It was Trump being Trump, the showman. Americans did not expect their films and television to be true. They did not expect Trump's words to be true. They did not expect anyone's words to be true, anymore.

Trump might have polled better in 2020 by being honest about what he had achieved, focusing on that, instead of lying about what he had not achieved. Being honest would have allowed him to explain his failures, inviting voters to let him try again a second time.

The difference between people supporting Trump in spite of his lies and dishonored promises and people supporting past presidents in spite of their lies and dishonored promises was one of degree. Eisenhower might not have considered that a significant difference.

8. PROMISES

Nationalists honor their promises to their compatriots. They also honor their promises to others, if the honor of their nation depends on it.

Individualists do not honor their promises to anyone, unless doing so suits them. It generally suits elected officials, at least those seeking re-election, to be seen to honor their promises.

Voters do not expect elected officials to honor all their promises, but they expect them to try. They expect them to honor their major promises.

Elected officials failing to honor their promises need to respect voters enough to explain their failure. Their explanation might be weak or implausible, but any excuse is better than none. Providing no explanation insults voters by deeming voters not worthy of explanation.

American presidents are normally elected because of broad policy objectives rather than specific policies. Most specific policies are small, only periodically in the public mind.

In 1980, Ronald Reagan's promises were big: to unwind the size of government, lower taxes, and balance the federal budget. Budget deficits soared during his presidency, but worrying about government accounts was something for nationalists.

Amidst the increasing individualism of the time, Reagan's integrity became less important. He honored his promise to cut personal taxes, which mattered more to voters, while the economy for them boomed.

In 1992, Bill Clinton promised to reform America's healthcare system to benefit the poor. As First Lady, Hillary Clinton worked hard to deliver it, but the Clintons could not get anything past the vested interests binding Congressional Democrats and Republicans.

Clinton pledged also to revive America's deteriorating inner cities. He did not.

Amidst postmodernism, people equate what they do to what

they say they do. Thus elected officials honor their promises by saying that they honor them. Voters decide for themselves whether they did, so far as they are concerned.

Presidential candidates' increasingly vague promises of bringing America together and the like made that easy. In 2000, George W Bush promised compassionate conservatism, as if conservatism otherwise was not. Islamic terror and the Iraq War superseded it.

In 2008, as well as healthcare reform, Barack Obama promised hope and change. Promises became self-fulfilling, in supporters' minds.

An exception was George H W Bush in 1988. "Read my lips," he told the Republican National Convention, "no new taxes." The promise was central to his campaign, retaining support from voters who supported Reagan before him.

In 1990, America's economic problems led to Bush agreeing a compromise budget agreement with the Democrat-controlled Congress that included no new taxes but that increased several existing taxes. *"It is clear to me,"* he said in a statement in June 1990, *"that both the size of the deficit problem and the need for a package that can be enacted require all of the following: entitlement and mandatory program reform, tax revenue increases, growth incentives, discretionary spending reductions, orderly reductions in defense expenditures, and budget process reform."*

Bush explained his decision in the national interest and could have argued that he had not broken his promise anyway, but the promise had been too important to his supporters for that. He failed to be re-elected in 1992.

Not since then had a presidential candidate made such an explicit promise so central to his election campaign as Trump made in 2016. "I will build a great, great wall on our southern border," Trump promised upon launching his campaign in June 2015, "and I'll have Mexico pay for that wall."

America's southern border was two thousand miles long. Time and again over the next year and a half, Trump repeated his promise to build a "big, beautiful wall," to the raucous adoration of his rallies. He did not ask voters to read his lips, because he made the promise so loudly and often.

Other countries, including Mexico, built walls along certain of their borders to prevent illegal immigration. Trump's wall would replace piecemeal patches of wall and fence already in place.

In February 2016, former Mexican president Vincente Fox said that Mexico was "not going to pay for that … wall."

"The wall just got ten feet taller, believe me," Trump responded at the Republican candidates' debate that evening in Houston. Trump later explained that Mexico would pay for the wall through new trade arrangements or the like.

Promising the wall might have won Trump the presidency. Within a week after his inauguration, he issued Executive Order 13767 to build "*a physical wall on the southern border.*" Late in 2017, the Department of Homeland Security constructed eight prototypes for the wall near San Diego. No longer a solid concrete wall, it was thirty-foot steel slats in sections.

Trump boasted of the wall being built, but in March 2019, the United States Customs and Border Protection reported that no new wall had been built. It had only repaired and replaced existing barriers.

Not since 1992 had a president so failed to honor a promise important to his supporters as Trump did. George H W Bush's excuse in 1990 for not honoring his 1988 promise was America's national interest. America's national interest was in Trump honoring his promise.

Not only was Trump not building a wall, he tried to stop others building it. In December 2019, at the request of the Trump administration, federal judge Randy Crane ordered Trump-supporting We Build the Wall and contractor Fisher Industries to cease construction of a three-mile long private border wall along the banks of the Rio Grande near Mission, Texas. A federal judge lifted the injunction in January 2020.

"*I disagreed with doing this very small (tiny) section of wall,*" tweeted Trump in July 2020, "*in a tricky area, by a private group which raised money by ads. It was only done to make me look bad, and perhaps it now doesn't even work. Should have been built like rest of Wall, 500 plus miles.*"

That was to say, Trump sued to stop private individuals building a border wall because it would embarrass him. The wall was not about America. It was about Trump.

He insisted that he was building the wall, while most work remained repairs and replacement of existing barriers. If Trump believed his exaggeration, then it harmed him further. It prevented him from correcting course, from seeing the damage to his re-election bid caused by the lack of a wall.

Was the wall something to promise for the applause it earned?

Was it a shallow superficial wish without conviction to sustain it in the face of challenges: a lazy mystical wanting dependent upon other people's work to build and Trump not being inconvenienced?

Trump did not talk of using the promise of a wall as a tactic to negotiate immigration reform, reducing legal and illegal immigration. Voters would have accepted achieving the wall's objectives by other means.

At the end of Trump's presidency, Customs and Border Protection reported that only forty-nine miles of new barrier had been built. In terms of the promise Trump made before the 2016 election, there was no wall.

In 2016, Trump's promise of a wall gave physical form to the nationalism he promised. In 2020, his failure to have built the wall expressed the emptiness of his nationalism. Individualism means that people feeling unharmed by immigration do not care about people most obviously harmed.

The wall was important because national borders are important. In 2016, Trump paraded before voters the Angel Families and Angel Moms, mourning loved ones dead because of illegal immigration. In his 2016 campaign and in office, Trump repeatedly pledged to deport millions of illegal immigrants.

In April 2018, the Department of Justice announced: "*Attorney General Jeff Sessions today notified all U.S. Attorney's Offices along the Southwest Border of a new "zero-tolerance policy" for offenses under 8 U.S.C. § 1325(a), which prohibits both attempted illegal entry and illegal entry into the United States by an alien.*"

There were no new laws. Attorney's Offices were simply going to enforce existing laws.

Accompanying criticism of Sessions' policy was news footage of illegal immigrant children detained in cages. "Those cages that were shown," Trump told reporters in the Oval Office in April 2018, "I think they were very inappropriate, they were built by President Obama's administration..."

Trump made Obama appear as good as he was on border protection. If illegal immigrants did not want their children caged, they should stay home. They could still return home.

Two months later, in June 2018, Trump hosted a White House event for fourteen relatives of eleven people killed by illegal immigrants. Also that month, Trump issued an executive order effectively ending Sessions' policy.

The Angel Families and Angel Moms were missing from Trump's 2020 campaign. Showcasing victims of illegal immigrants would only remind voters that those illegal immigrants remained in America.

Trump's course was the worst course: deriding illegal immigrants, but failing to deport them. It alienated American globalists and Latino nationalists without return.

America would have been better, and Trump's re-election prospects better, if he had spoken politely of illegal immigrants while deporting them all. He might have absorbed less hatred from his opponents, while protecting America and Americans.

Before Trump, Republican presidents were normally generous to illegal immigrants, unconcerned about Americans. In 1986, President Reagan granted amnesty to three million illegal immigrants, which in 1990 President George H W Bush extended to more illegal immigrants.

"It backfired big-time," California governor Schwarzenegger, another Republican, told the Spanish-language Univision television network in October 2005. "It sent the wrong message: You come here illegally, and then we go and give you amnesty. So then, the next million come and they say, 'Hey, we get amnesty, this is really terrific'."

The 1992 election might have been the reason that in May 1992, George H W Bush ordered the interception and immediate repatriation to Haiti of Haitians coming by boat. Catering to different voters, Democrat nominee Bill Clinton initially opposed Bush's order, promising instead to consider each Haitian's claim for refugee status. Shortly before his inauguration, Clinton said he would maintain Bush's order.

In 2012, Obama announced his Deferred Action for Childhood Arrivals program. It allowed illegal immigrants brought to America as children to receive a renewable two-year period of deferred action from deportation and become eligible for a work permit, provided they had no felonies or serious misdemeanors on their criminal records. Lesser criminals were fine.

Obama sought to expand the program in 2014, until litigation from several states thwarted the expansion. An evenly divided Supreme Court blocked the expansion. In June 2017, Trump rescinded the expansion.

In September 2017, Trump announced that he was phasing out the program, but deferred that phase out while Congress considered immigration reform, including laws granting illegal immigrants paths to citizenship: another amnesty. Congress did not pass such laws, but court decisions prevented Trump's rescission taking effect.

In June 2020, the Supreme Court by a single vote overturned Trump's rescission, but on grounds that allowed him another chance to rescind the program. A presidential election that year was no reason not to try again to rescind it. The election was a reason to try again to rescind it, which Trump did not take.

In 2016, immigration defined Trump's campaign. People loved Trump for his immigration policies. Other people hated Trump for his immigration rhetoric. How popular might his policies have been, if they came without the inflammatory rhetoric?

Without talk of race or religion, David Cameron in Britain in 2010 and Jacinda Ardern in New Zealand in 2017 were elected with promises to cut immigration. With Trump, they formed a small chorus of political candidates promising a return to traditional nationalism from the political left and political right. All three failed to provide it in office.

H-1B visas allowed American employers to employ lower paid foreign workers, replacing higher paid American workers. Often, the Americans' last task before departing their jobs was training the immigrants replacing them.

"*I will end forever the use of the H-1B as a cheap labor program,*" declared Trump in a press release in March 2016, "*and institute an absolute requirement to hire American workers first for every visa and immigration program. No exceptions.*"

Soon after the election, in December 2016, senior representatives of America's big technology companies courted Trump in Trump Tower, New York, asking that he expand the availability of H-1B visas. Trump agreed to do so, as he told media baron Rupert Murdoch later that day in a telephone conversation described in Michael Wolff's 2018 book *Fire and Fury*. Murdoch pointed out that expanding the availability of H-1B visas conflicted with Trump's promises before the election.

"We'll figure it out," answered Trump.

"What a ... idiot," said Murdoch, hanging up his telephone.

In April 2017, Trump signed an executive order for federal

agencies to "Buy American, Hire American." Meanwhile, temporary working visas increased by five percent each year through Trump's presidency to 2019, according to the Department of Homeland Security. Only in 2020, amidst the pandemic, did Trump restrict H-1B visas.

Amidst contradictory messages from Trump, he spoke most in favor of recalibrating American immigration laws towards a merit-based approach, restricting immigration to well-educated, law-abiding, healthy immigrants skilled in jobs useful to America. He spoke against existing immigration avenues.

President Johnson, a Democrat, replaced national origin quotas with skilled immigration and chain migration in the Immigration and Nationality Act of 1965. Chain migration allowed immigrants to bring their endless chains of relatives to America, inadvertently spurring interracial immigration. In September 1965, a greater proportion of Senate Republicans than Democrats voted in favor of the law.

The visa lottery sought to increase racial and religious diversity in America by offering visas to countries from which relatively few immigrants came. In October 2017, an Uzbek immigrant on a diversity visa killed eight people and injured eleven on a sidewalk in Lower Manhattan, leading Trump to call for an end to the program.

"Chain migration is a disaster, and very unfair to our country," said Trump during a weekly address in February 2018. "The visa lottery is something that should have never been allowed in the first place. People enter a lottery to come into our country. What kind of a system is that? It is time for Congress to act and to protect Americans."

In August 2017, Congress considered the Reforming American Immigration for Strong Employment Act, the RAISE Act, which sought to reduce legal immigration and set conditions for accepting immigrants over ten years. Trump invited Stephen Miller to argue the case for the Act to the White House press corps.

Miller had been Jeff Sessions' communications director when Sessions was in the Senate. He then became a senior adviser to Trump throughout Trump's presidency, as was Trump's son-in-law Jared Kushner. In December 2018, sociologist Gordon Fellman declared *"Jared Kushner and Stephen Miller Are the Most Assimilated Jews in America."*

Trump's partial ban upon Muslims was accredited to Miller, as was Trump cutting refugee admissions. Cutting the refugee intake was relatively easy, much as past administrations found admitting refugees to be easy.

Miller's expertise was immigration, although in April 2017, *Politico* reported that Miller "*is now working closely with Kushner's Office of American Innovation, as well as on family leave, child care and women's issues with Kushner's wife, Ivanka Trump, according to several people involved.*"

The RAISE Act did not pass. Chain migration and the visa lottery did not end.

In November 2018, Trump announced that he would issue an executive order to ensure that anchor babies born in America to illegal immigrants or birthing tourists did not obtain birthright citizenship pursuant to the Fourteenth Amendment of the American Constitution. He never did.

In September 2019, Trump issued a proclamation restricting chain migration. In Oregon, district judge Michael Simon prevented the proclamation taking effect, pending the outcome of other court action against the proclamation.

In April 2020, amidst the pandemic, Trump signed an executive order "temporarily suspending immigration into the United States," he said. The order included so many exemptions as to be almost meaningless.

"This announcement is more about grabbing a headline than changing immigration policy," America's Voice executive director Frank Sharry told *Associated Press*.

Trump took some measures to curtail immigration, but most of his important 2016 election promises remained unfulfilled. If he had been mistaken to make those promises, he did not say so.

He did not say that he changed his mind and give his reasons for changing. Voters could then have judged him on those reasons.

If Trump had excuses for not honoring those promises, he did not provide them. Excuses could have mitigated his failure.

Instead, Trump treated voters with disdain. What remained for his supporters was the hope that, however little Trump did on immigration, he would still be better than a Democrat.

In October 2020, Stephen Miller told *NBC News* of several measures to cut immigration that he would seek to implement if Trump were re-elected. If Trump's first term had implemented those measures, there might have been a second term.

9. NECESSARY ENEMIES

Sometimes in life, people cannot help but make enemies. They might be espousing morality in the face of the immoral. They might be espousing facts in the face of the fanciful.

"You have enemies?" wrote French novelist Victor Hugo in his essay 'Villemain' in 1845. *"Why, it is the story of every man who has done a great deed or created a new idea. It is the cloud which thunders around everything that shines. Fame must have enemies, as light must have gnats. Do not bother yourself about it; disdain. Keep your mind serene as you keep your life clear."*

Hugo's words might have given rise to a quote attributed to British wartime leader Winston Churchill, although there is no record that Churchill ever said it. *"You have enemies? Good. That means you've stood up for something, sometime in your life."*

In public office, elected officials doing what they think is right can make enemies of other people also doing what they think is right. Played sensitively, respectively towards those enemies, those enemies might be minimized. Their hostility might be minimized.

Nationalists cannot help but make enemies of people opposed to their nation. Those enemies might oppose all nations or only their nation, but they oppose it nevertheless.

Foremost among those opposed to American nationalism is the mainstream media. The corporate press expresses the views of corporate America.

Like other Americans by 2015, mainstream journalists knew only people like them, at work and away from work. While other Americans knew the beliefs and attitudes of mainstream media figures because they saw, heard, and read those beliefs and attitudes every day, those mainstream media figures had no such eyes or ears for the beliefs and attitudes of people beyond their social boundaries.

If mainstream media figures listened to the radio, it was not for the listeners' talkback or opinions of program hosts with whom they disagreed. If they used social media, they posted more than they read, except of people like them.

They thus had every reason to see Trump as an aberration, a freak, who surely did not believe what he said about immigration and Islam. There was no question that Trump would lose the 2016 election because few people thought as he thought, or spoke as he spoke.

Trump did not simply shock mainstream journalists and their friends. He fascinated them. Trump secured media attention as no other presidential candidate did.

The Never-Trump Republicans

Foes from outside politicians' political parties are one thing. Political candidates expect them. Foes from within their parties are much more difficult.

Churchill remained in the House of Commons until 1955. A newly elected young member was reputed to have taken a place on the parliamentary benches and, pointing to the benches opposite, said to Churchill, "So that's the enemy."

"No, son," Churchill is reputed to have replied. "That's the opposition." He then pointed to the benches behind them and their fellow Conservative Party members. "That is the enemy."

The same could be said of Trump and some members of the Republican Party. From its inception, the Republican Party had been dominated by the rich and powerful. Aside perhaps from a few periods of respite, most notably under Newt Gingrich in the 1990s, the Republican Party had a long history of disinterest in poor and working class people. Nevertheless, Democrats increasingly embracing other races from the 1960s left the Republican Party as the lesser of two unsavory options for poor white Americans. In 2016 and 2020, Gingrich supported Trump.

Among the reasons to support Trump in 2016 and throughout his presidency were the people who most opposed him. That was not Democrats, for America had become accustomed to Democrats and Republicans hating each other. The better the Republican, the more Democrats hated him or her.

It was Republicans. Never before in living memory had a nominee produced such public opposition from within his or her political party as Trump did.

The Never-Trump Republicans were much like Trump's critics from among Democrats, except that they were Republicans. They were generally conservative and globalist.

As the Republican Party nominee for president in 2012, Mitt Romney appeared to be a non-ideological candidate, willing to work with Democrats and Republicans alike. With a background in management consulting, especially aiding the organizing of the 2002 Winter Olympic Games in Salt Lake City, the former Governor of Massachusetts offered much.

Romney displayed his centrist pragmatism in response to calls to deport illegal immigrants. "The answer is self-deportation," he said in the Republican candidates' debate in Tampa in January 2012, "which is people decide they can do better by going home because they can't find work here, because they don't have legal documentation to allow them to work here..."

If he was elected president in 2012, Romney would create conditions in which illegal immigrants would willingly return home. Without the financial, educational, medical, and other incentives that Western countries provide people to immigrate and remain, fewer of them would come and fewer of them would stay, legally or illegally.

In 2012, Trump endorsed Romney, but in a speech at the University of Utah in March 2016, Romney rebuked Trump. "Donald Trump is a phony, a fraud," said Romney. "His promises are as worthless as a degree from Trump University. He's playing the American public for suckers: He gets a free ride to the White House and all we get is a lousy hat."

Romney did not oppose Trump for being a phony. *"Today,"* Romney wrote on his Facebook page in March 2016, *"there is a contest between Trumpism and Republicanism. Through the calculated statements of its leader, Trumpism has become associated with racism, misogyny, bigotry, xenophobia, vulgarity and, most recently, threats and violence. I am repulsed by each and every one of these."*

Mormons are reputedly sensitive to racial and religious discrimination because they feel they have been victims of religious discrimination. Romney was a Mormon.

For past Republican nominees not to support Trump was a rebuff not simply to Trump. It was a smack in the face to loyal Republicans who supported them in their general election after not supporting them in their primaries and caucuses.

After Trump secured the Republican Party nomination in 2016, Romney declared that he would not vote for Trump or Hillary Clinton on Election Day. In 2018, Romney revealed that he voted for a write-in candidate: his wife, Ann Romney.

While other Never-Trump Republicans continued their public opposition to Trump after his election in 2016, Romney respected that election and supported him. Trump endorsed Romney in the Utah Senate election of 2018.

Romney publicly criticized Trump whenever he saw fit. At Trump's first trial before the Senate early in 2020, Romney became the first American senator in history to vote to convict a president of his own party, when he did so in respect of one of the two charges.

He did not vote for Trump in the 2020 election. That Romney was among the seven Republicans voting to convict Trump at his second trial before the Senate, in February 2021, surprised no one.

Other Never-Trump Republicans were at least as concerned about Trump's foreign policy, especially his talk of bringing American troops home from foreign wars and his refusal to start or join more wars. What was the point of the American military if not to kill American servicemen and women?

Editor of *The Weekly Standard* magazine, Jewish conservative Bill Kristol had long supported America invading Iraq before she finally did in 2003. "*It's Our War,*" Kristol wrote of the Lebanon War in 2006, "*Bush should go to Jerusalem – and the U.S. should confront Iran.*"

People vehemently opposed to Trump could be more horrible than he was. "Look," Kristol told an American Enterprise Institute event in February 2017, "to be totally honest, if things are so bad as you say with the white working class, don't you want to get new Americans in?" He saw America's racial replacement as good for business. "Basically if you are in free society, a capitalist society, after two, three, four generations of hard work, everyone becomes kind of decadent, lazy, spoiled, whatever."

America's poor and middle classes did not feel decadent, lazy, or spoiled. They had seen their lives and America deteriorate over the preceding decades and dared to care about that deterioration. Kristol did not.

Foes of American nationalism do not need to be ideological. They can be people making money and otherwise profiting at

America's expense. Protecting and aiding America's poor can make enemies of people who feel they lose by the process.

Among Trump's most popular promises in 2016 was to drain the swamp: to rid Washington of the elite self-serving sectional interests that had neglected America for so long. Behind partisan politics, the rich and powerful cozied up with whomever was president and whichever party controlled Congress. Since presidencies and control of Congress could change, they remained close to the elite of both major parties. Aspiring politicians became close to the elite so they could join it.

The swamp was Democrat and Republican. It was not just congressmen and women, but also the lobbyists that fed them, corporate and globalist interests that funded them, and aides who fed from them. It was bureaucrats living well from the money paid to the federal government in taxes, and every big business syphoning off some of those riches for themselves.

Poor and vulnerable people need nationalism from more than their elected officials. They need nationalism from bureaucrats.

Cleaning out Washington had been a common catch cry since President Reagan's first inauguration address in 1981, when he declared "government is not the solution to our problem, government is the problem." In 1996, cinema audiences watching the film *Independence Day* cheered to see the White House exploding.

Drawing its name from the Boston Tea Party of 1773 and later said to mean "taxed enough already," the Tea Party movement formed in 2009 in response to the expanding role of government under President Obama. It sought to clean up Washington and attracted considerable success in the 2010 mid-term Congressional elections, not just for ordinary Americans becoming congressmen and women but for influencing other congressmen and women.

Opposition to Washington was central to Joni Ernst's successful Iowa Senate campaign in 2014. She gained wide renown for a television commercial featuring pigs, with her promise to make Washington squeal.

Few of those elected congressmen and women achieved very much. They succumbed to elite sectional interests, joining them.

Nor did Trump drain the swamp. If Washington did not change Trump, it was because he already stood in the swamp.

Draining the swamp was something more for Congressional leaderships, although Trump seeking Congressional support to implement his promises would have clarified voters' choices at the next Congressional election. Only voters at Congressional elections can drain the Congressional swamp.

If Trump and his appointees could not secure nationalism from bureaucrats, they should have appointed bureaucrats from whom they could secure it. Trump could have filled Washington's bureaucracy with American nationalism. He did not.

In defense of Trump were claims that he was being thwarted by the Deep State. Like the establishment, elites, and classes of people, the Deep State was an imprecise term describing a type of person, who might or might not have considered himself or herself as such. Those people were not formal members of anything and need have no knowledge of or interaction with each other.

They were the people in government roles, or other roles presumably, maintaining the sectional corporatist or other globalist policies against which Trump railed and that he had been elected to curtail or expunge. If the swamp was the obvious players in Washington, then the Deep State was people hiding in the swamp, maintaining an agenda against the interests of the American people.

Deep State operatives did not need to be rich. They could be ideological. They were the appointees under previous presidents, when American government had become increasingly ideological and self-serving.

They might not have even existed, but they were Trump's supporters' excuses for Trump achieving so little. If they were real, Trump in office could have tried to persuade them to nationalism or to implement his agenda for being their job to implement it. If Trump could not do that, then he could fire them. He fired plenty of people.

It was easy to believe there was no Deep State, until September 2018 when *The New York Times* newspaper published the article 'I Am Part of the Resistance inside the Trump Administration,' by the self-styled Anonymous. *"This isn't the work of the so-called deep state,"* wrote Anonymous, a traditional Republican who supported Trump's taxation policy but opposed his foreign policy. *"It's the work of the steady state."* In 2019, Anonymous published the book *A Warning.*

Shortly before the 2020 election, after previously denying he was Anonymous, Miles Taylor revealed himself. An appointee of President George W Bush, the lifelong member of the Republican

Party was also an appointee under Trump, becoming deputy chief of staff to Secretary Kirstjen Nielsen and Acting Secretary Kevin McAleenan at the Department of Homeland Security.

The Deep State was real, although its practical impact remained unclear. It was as much a consequence of the poor appointments Trump made in office as a legacy from the past.

Taylor thought he was harming Trump's re-election prospects by his thread of twenty-five tweets early in November 2020, revealing instructions that Trump had given the Department of Homeland Security during Taylor's time there. *"Trump told us: Let's cut the number of refugees we let into the United States to ZERO,"* said one tweet. *"They don't add anything to our country and are a drain on our welfare system."* If more people had seen Taylor's tweets, Trump might have been re-elected.

Republicans who hated Trump in 2016 for his talk of nationalism still hated him. Nobody worked harder than the Never-Trump Republicans to remove Trump from office in 2020.

Some Never-Trump Republicans wanted to bring down the Republican Party altogether, presumably allowing them to restore it to the party that President George W Bush made it. *"Conservatives need to put the current Republican Party out of its – and our – misery,"* wrote conservative academic Tom Nichols in September 2020.

Trump's critics talked and wrote of Trump, watched and read of him, more than most of his supporters did. Otherwise rational and reasonable people could be consumed by him, as most of Trump's supporters were not.

More telling than the incessant Never-Trump Republicans were those who ceased. Some conservatives warmed to Trump from 2016 to 2020.

Glenn Beck was a Roman Catholic who became a Mormon. "We all look at Adolf Hitler in 1940," said Beck on the television program *This Week* early in March 2016. "We should look at Adolf Hitler in 1929. He was a kind of a funny kind of character that said the things people were thinking. Where Donald Trump takes it, I have absolutely no idea, but Donald Trump is a dangerous man with the things that he has been saying."

In May 2018, Beck donned a red *"Make America Great Again"* cap and declared of Trump on *The Glenn Beck Radio Program*: "I'll vote for him in 2020." Among the reasons Beck gave was Trump's record in office.

Ben Shapiro was a practicing Jew. "I did not vote for Donald Trump in 2016," said Shapiro on *The Ben Shapiro Show* in October 2020. "I am voting for Donald Trump in 2020." He set out three reasons, including: "Donald Trump has governed pretty conservatively."

They were not persuaded to support Trump by arguments in support of nationalism. Smart enough to focus upon the reality instead of the rhetoric, they saw not a nationalist presidency, but a conservative one.

"And by the way," Shapiro tweeted in June 2017, *"I don't give a good damn about the so-called "browning of America." Color doesn't matter. Ideology does."*

Conservatism had become, for some, no less a globalist ideology than communism: uninterested in race, culture, and people, but consumed with what people believed, as if beliefs could be separated from race and culture. Conservatives like Shapiro could thus be similar to liberals like James Carville, a Democrat. Shapiro called ideology what Carville called an idea. They were both ideological definitions of America, as she was or as he wanted her to be, although ideologies opposed to each other.

A problem with defining countries by ideas and ideologies is that people cannot agree upon what those ideas and ideologies are, or should be. Shapiro and Carville would not have agreed.

The globalism that redefined American conservatism and liberalism by 2016 would have made them both alien to America through her first two hundred years. From her founding until the middle of the twentieth century, America was unashamedly nationalist, even where and when that nation was the Confederacy.

White people's values are not those of other races; nor are Jewish values. Diversity and inclusion are not conservative; nor were they classically liberal.

Like Brexit in Britain with the Conservative Party, Trump had a chance to move the Republican Party from conservatism to nationalism, recognizing that races have cultures and cultures include beliefs. Trump brought conservatism back towards a nationalist conservatism more in his oratory than his performance.

Trump might have won the 2020 election had his presidency remained opposed by Beck and Shapiro. Trump's conservatism in office might not have delivered him enough additional support among conservatives to overcome any electoral support he lost among Americans not so conservative, but who voted for him in 2016 for the nationalism he promised and perhaps even the racism he exuded, without then seeing enough practical nationalism during his presidency.

10. UNNECESSARY ENEMIES

Critics are not enemies. They might simply be people who disagree.

Critics might be supporters. They might simply recognize a person's errors and failings.

People might lose allies over time by holding fast to their cause, religion, or people, when others do not. They might lose allies by not holding fast, when others do.

Trump's necessary enemies were people opposed to American nationalism, because of the promises he made. His unnecessary enemies were people supporting American nationalism, because of his failure to honor those promises.

Most of Trump's supporters did not brandish signs and flags for him. They went about their lives: trying to earn income, keeping their families, and playing. They also watched and read the news.

Many Americans voting for Trump in 2016 already recognized the benefits of American nationalism to them and the people for whom they cared, even if they did not think of it as being nationalism. Other Americans needed reasons or at least assurance for their nationalism. They found those reasons and assurance in a small minority of dissident news and opinion media, among experts and commentators aiding the nationalist cause.

Matt Drudge founded the *Drudge Report* website in 1995. Primarily a news aggregation service, Drudge gained worldwide renown in January 1998 for breaking news of President Clinton's relationship with Monica Lewinsky, after *Newsweek* magazine declined to publish the story.

"I'm a libertarian, except for drugs and abortion," Drudge, a Jew reputedly not practicing, told Robert Scheer in July 1998. "I'm a conservative…" he told *The Sunday Times* newspaper in April 2005, "but I'm more of a populist." Populism of the political right and traditionally of the political left is nationalism.

A consummate newshound, Drudge had possibly the keenest nose for news in America. While the mainstream press treated race as immaterial, Drudge understood that normal people care about their race becoming a minority in the country their forebears built, and to which they were born.

While the mainstream press could not imagine a link between Islam and terror, ordinary people saw the link. The terrorists declared it.

By disseminating information that mainstream news services did not, Drudge and other dissident journalists and publishers laid the groundwork for Trump's candidacy in 2015. They were the imparters of facts upon which Trump would rely. So when Trump in 2015 spoke of trade, immigration, and Islam as ordinary people did, Drudge being a newsman reported it.

"A large measure of why Trump is the nominee goes to Matt Drudge," veteran reporter Carl Bernstein told CNN in July 2016. "Drudge is really the great new factor in terms of media."

In March 2017, Drudge made a rare public appearance on Michael Savage's radio program *The Savage Nation*. "Since when did the president become someone who was in your face daily?" asked Drudge, supporting Trump but questioning why Trump remained so visible. "I think we would respect him if he got serious things done, and the end result, you judge the tree by the fruit."

By then commanding attention more from others than from Drudge, Trump talked, and tweeted, and talked a lot, with little useful and new to say. He got few serious things done.

"Drudge is great, by the way," Trump told Steve Doocy on the *Fox & Friends* television program in June 2018. "Matt Drudge is a great gentleman, who really has an ability to capture the stories that people want to see."

Drudge might or might not have changed in 2019. Being privately owned, the ownership, management, and funding of the *Drudge Report* remained unknown to the public. Whatever the change that occurred to its business model that year, Drudge appeared to retain control over the *Drudge Report*. The private-natured Drudge has not revealed otherwise.

Trump had certainly changed since 2016. "*NO NEW WALL AT ALL!*" declared the *Drudge Report* in July 2019. In spite of Trump's claims that he was building a border wall with Mexico, Drudge referred readers to a *Washington Examiner* magazine report that the only money spent was spent replacing sections of existing fencing.

Drudge had long reported facts that Trump needed reporting

when other media players did not. Drudge's fault was reporting facts when facts were not so favorable to Trump.

Reports, not on Drudge, were that Trump felt Drudge had turned against him, but Trump recognized that nobody told Drudge what to say. Trump spoke of him having previously fallen out of favor with Drudge when he felt he was back in favor. When the facts again spoke poorly of Trump, as far as those issues so dear to normal people were concerned, Drudge again reported it.

In April 2020, Trump retweeted a claim that Drudge's coverage of the pandemic was misleading and sensationalist. *"I gave up on Drudge (a really nice guy) long ago, as have many others,"* added Trump. *"People are dropping like flies!"*

Drudge made a rare personal statement in his defense. *"The past 30 days has been the most eyeballs in Drudge Report's 26 year-history,"* he wrote, in an email to CNN. *"Heartbreaking that it has been under such tragic circumstances."*

The newsman Drudge might simply have sensed something in people's mood. "Matt Drudge is first and foremost a businessman and a brilliant one," Matthew Lysiak, author of *The Drudge Revolution*, told Axios Media in July 2020. "His interest is not in political loyalties. It's in page hits."

Through the course of 2020, Drudge began reporting stories that seemed to have no other purpose than to damage Trump. In September 2020, the *Drudge Report* banner headline was *"TRUMP DENIES MINI-STROKE SENT HIM TO HOSPITAL."*

By reporting denials, truthful news can plant ideas in people's minds that they otherwise would not have had. Similar headlines from Drudge might have harmed Hillary Clinton in 2016.

Leaders failing to lead invite conflicts among people who ought to be allies. Radio host Mark Levin tweeted a copy of Drudge's mini-stroke banner, with the caption: *"Drudge at it again. Promoting crackpot New York Times "reporter" and his book trashing Trump."*

As if to prove that he did not need friends, Trump turned ever more harshly on Drudge. *"Drudge didn't support me in 2016,"* Trump replied to Levin's tweet, *"and I hear he doesn't support me now. Maybe that's why he is doing poorly. His Fake News report on Mini-Strokes is incorrect. Possibly thinking about himself, or the other party's "candidate"."*

Drudge did support Trump in 2016. The *Drudge Report* had long reported the number of daily, monthly, and annual visits to the site. They numbered more than ten billion in the preceding year.

The issues important to Drudge in 2020 were important to him in 2016. They were important to his readers.

Late in October 2010, only days before the election, Drudge reported "*OBAMA DEPORTED MORE ILLEGALS...*" Pointing to Trump's inactivity on the signature pitch of his 2016 campaign, the headline linked to a report from *The Hill*, which quoted a report from *The Washington Post* newspaper, both reports almost a year old.

If Drudge was proving that Trump should have given him some credit for his victory in 2016, then he succeeded. Trump lost in 2020.

The stories hostile to Trump, sometimes unfairly, continued after the election. A November 2020 story headlined with the Pfizer pharmaceutical company not being part of the Trump administration's Warp Speed response to the pandemic linked to a story saying that the company had been part of the response, but it had not taken government funds.

Drudge might not have been content for Trump to have lost in 2020. He might have been ensuring Trump could not win in 2024.

With some of his former supporters, Trump inspired bitterness in their opposition much like the bitterness with which he turned upon people. Having realized that Trump as president would not carry out the promises upon which they first assisted him, there was no loss in opposing him.

Drudge let the news he presented on the *Drudge Report* speak for itself, without word from Drudge beyond a banner or by-line. Commentator Ann Coulter spoke. She wrote. She tweeted.

For years, Coulter had been a consistent critic of the immigration ruining America. She had the patriotism to care and nationalism to write her 2015 book *¡Adios, America!* Like Drudge, Coulter laid groundwork for Trump's candidacy.

A credible candidate for president, Trump seemed like a champion to save Americans from immigration. Three days after Trump announced his candidacy, Bill Maher on the *Real Time with Bill Maher* television program asked Coulter which of the candidates had the best chance of winning the Republican Party nomination. "Of the declared ones," answered Coulter, "right now, Donald Trump." The Los Angeles live audience laughed.

People make heroes and heroines of people who fight for them. From nationalism come heroes and heroines, personifying the nation. In 2016, Coulter published *In Trump We Trust*, subtitled *E*

Pluribus Awesome!

Reciprocating her regard, Coulter was a rare person that Trump followed on Twitter. That more than anything else demonstrated the regard he held for her opinion.

Coulter never changed. Trump changed.

In September 2017, Trump tweeted his support for illegal immigrants he had promised to deport before the 2016 election. *"They have been in our country for many years through no fault of their own – brought in by parents at young age."*

"At this point," Coulter tweeted in reply, *"who DOESN'T want Trump impeached."*

Coulter repeatedly called upon Trump to honor the promises he made before the 2016 election, especially but not only his promises to cut immigration. "They're about to have a country where no Republican will ever be elected president again," she told *The Daily Caller* in December 2018. "Trump will just have been a joke presidency who scammed the American people, amused the populists for a while, but he'll have no legacy whatsoever."

In response, Trump ceased following her on Twitter. For a man as wedded to Twitter as was Trump, but who followed only forty-five people after ceasing to follow Coulter, that was the social media equivalent of banishing her to a prison tower.

Coulter continued to challenge Trump to exercise the power of his office, when he preferred to tweet. In January 2019, the Federal Bureau of Investigation arrested Trump's informal adviser Roger Stone at his home in Florida. *CNN News* cameras were there to record the arrest.

"Who alerted CNN to be there?" asked Trump in a tweet.

"Trump tweets about Roger Stone raid," tweeted Coulter. *"'Who alerted CNN to be there?' Just think! If you were president, you could haul the FBI director's ass into the Oval Office and ask him yourself."*

Trump continued to lie. *"Wacky Nut Job @AnnCoulter,"* Trump tweeted in March 2019, *"who still hasn't figured out that, despite all odds and an entire Democrat Party of Far Left Radicals against me (not to mention certain Republicans who are sadly unwilling to fight), I am winning on the Border. Major sections of Wall are being built..."*

More than her reputation was always the substance of what Coulter said. Had Trump in power demonstrated that he too was a nationalist of conviction, Coulter would have retained her trust in Trump. So would more voters than those who did.

In May 2020, Coulter responded to Trump's most recent tweet against the loyal Jeff Sessions by tweeting of Trump: *"The most disloyal actual retard that has ever set foot in the Oval Office is trying to lose AND take the Senate with him."* Her words were prophetic.

That month, Coulter told *Yahoo News* that instead of voting for Trump in 2020, she will "probably write in Jeff Sessions." To whatever extent she aided Trump in 2016, she sowed doubt among people who might have voted for him again in 2020, or turned those people against him.

Trump inspired great devotion in people who never met him. He could inspire great hostility among people who had.

With so much of the mainstream media against him, and with Trump burning off supporters in the dissident media and elsewhere, the mass of loud opinion became ever more hostile towards him. He needed supporters more in 2020 than he needed them in 2016.

The remarkable feature of Trump's presidency was not the enemies he made by his treatment of his supporters, but that more of those supporters he maltreated did not turn against him. Men like Jeff Sessions and Chris Christie had reason to turn against him but did not, although Christie commenting for *ABC News* criticized Trump on matters of policy and messaging. Christie condemned Trump for inciting his supporters to storm the Capitol Building in January 2021.

Trump had few friends in politics and the media early in his campaign for the 2016 election. Quite apart from the practicalities of the 2020 election, it is extraordinary at a personal and moral level that he should have come to treat those friends he did have so badly.

Anyone trying to change or save a country needs supporters. Political candidates need supporters. The higher the office they seek, the more supporters they need.

To turn upon supporters because a person is certain that he or she does not need those supporters is not the actions of a nationalist, or anyone else committed to a cause, religion, or people. It is the actions of an individualist.

It is not just arrogant and nasty. It is stupid. It invites circumstances to arise in which a person needs that support no longer there.

No elected official can betray his supporters like Trump did during his presidency and expect to win re-election. Might Trump have won in 2020 with Drudge republishing favorable stories, or at least not republishing so many negative stories? Might he have won with Coulter commenting in his support, perhaps writing another book?

Perhaps, although no words that people spoke, wrote, or published mattered as much as Trump's performance in office. The reasons that Trump lost support from Drudge and Coulter were more important than losing that support.

11. CONSERVATISM

Nationalism is not conservatism. Conservatism can be nationalist, but so can liberalism, socialism, and anything else. They can also be globalist. They can also be individualist.

For the 2016 election, Trump's candidacy was founded upon nationalism, but he also claimed conservatism. "When you get down to it," he told the *Morning Joe* television program in August 2015, "I am a conservative person. I am by nature a somewhat conservative person." His presidency spoke the rhetoric of nationalism and conservatism, but the delivery was primarily in conservatism.

Conservatism differs between cultures, places, and times. President Reagan redefined American conservatism in the 1980s to become increasingly globalist as regards foreign policy, defense, immigration, and trade.

Becoming ever more individualist regarding economics, American conservatism became something for rich people. Trickle-down economics imagined rich people getting richer eventually enriching poor people. It did not happen.

Nationalism is for everyone. Sometimes, rich people missing out on a little mean poor people getting a lot, so the nation is better off overall. A dollar means more to a poor man than to a rich man.

To aid the poor, nationalism supports minimum wage increases. To aid the rich, conservatism opposes minimum wage increases. Trump vacillated on the issue, while the federal minimum wage remained low through his term in office.

Trump added to the nationalist tinge left in American conservatism, but it remained just a tinge. For Trump to laud rising stock markets through much of his presidency was to gloss over Wall Street being only one segment of the American economy. Stock prices can boom because whole economies boom, because only big corporations listed on stock exchanges boom, or because money needs somewhere to be.

Income tax cuts had long been Republican instincts if not

enactments. They could be useful for people who received them, but not so useful for people who did not.

Nationalism requires taxpayers to pay as little taxes as they must in the circumstances, but they normally must pay some. Nationalist income tax cuts favor the poor and middle classes, to the extent the poor pay taxes. Nationalism cares enough for future generations to balance government accounts over time, so does not cut income taxes for people today that add to the taxes that their children and grandchildren pay.

Trump's Tax Cuts and Jobs Act of 2017 cut taxes. It worsened America's budget deficit, as tax cuts normally do.

Before his election, Trump promised to end the carried interest tax loophole, which allowed the managers of hedge funds and private equity funds, including billionaires, to pay the lower capital gains tax rate rather than their higher income tax rate on their shares of fund profits. In 2013, the Congressional Budget Office estimated that it would give them seventeen billion dollars over the ensuing decade. In December 2017, the White House chief economic advisor Gary Cohn said hedge funds and private equity stopped Congress from cutting the loophole. "*Hedge fund tax loophole shows 'swamp' still rules over Washington, D.C.*," reported CNBC.

One element of Trump's tax reform was nationalistic. Trump capped to ten thousand dollars taxpayer deductions for payments of state and local taxes from their payments of federal income taxes. It was a tax imposition from which people paying less than ten thousand dollars in state and local taxes were spared.

State and local taxes should never have been deductions in the first place. In general terms, high-taxing states, cities, and counties provided more benefits in return. Granting those taxpayers relief from federal taxes meant that they suffered no expense for the benefits they received.

Voters were left unconcerned about their state and local taxes. The normal accountability of state and local governments was absent.

The federal government still needed revenue. Thus taxpayers paying less state and local taxes effectively subsidized taxpayers paying more state and local taxes, without receiving the benefits the latter received.

For poor and middle-class Americans, conservatism was more a matter of social policy. With the American North to the political left of the American South, the more socially conservative Southern Democrats were more to America's overall center than Northern Democrats were. After liberal Massachusetts governor Michael Dukakis' loss in 1988, many Democrats felt that a Northern Democrat could not become president.

In January 1992, Arkansas governor Bill Clinton had no legal reason to suspend his presidential election campaign to return to Little Rock for the execution of dual murderer Ricky Ray Rector, but doing so drew voters' attention to Clinton's support for the death penalty, with no chance of him pardoning a condemned man during an election campaign. It also drew voters' attention away from allegations that Clinton had carried on an adulterous affair with Gennifer Flowers. In November 1992, America elected Clinton president.

Revealed to the world in 1998, Clinton's infidelity with Monica Lewinsky harmed people's impressions of Clinton as a husband and father. They did not affect people's perceptions of him as a successful president.

Worse in the public mind than Clinton's infidelity were his political adversaries talking about it. That disrespected Clinton's wife, daughter, and the precious institute of marriage. Citing Clinton's infidelity in the campaign for the 1998 mid-term Congressional elections cost the Republican Party seats, when it expected to gain seats. There remained a general sense that private immorality should remain private.

Voters shared Republican views on morality, but did not want to hear them so often. If Democrats needed to nominate a Southerner, then perhaps Republicans needed to nominate a Northerner: someone without a Southern focus on moral issues. In the context of everything else, the result was again America's political center.

Trump was a New Yorker. When he announced his campaign in June 2015, his long record of tweeting and other commentary suggested little interest in social and moral issues.

Morality did not used to be conservative. It did not used to be reserved to Christians of faith.

Instead, nationalism underpinned morality, for people caring about their compatriots. Immorality is individualism, as is tolerance of immorality.

While adultery remained immoral, propaganda persuaded many Americans to give up other morals. Normal people saw worsening moral degradation and lunacy.

Adulterers kept their immorality secret. Homosexuals paraded theirs in the street.

Normal Americans might have tolerated other people's perversions in private bedrooms, but did not want to hear about them. The presumption of private bedrooms was that people in public did not have to know what happened there.

Normal people knew men from women. There was something insane about a man thinking that he was a woman or a woman thinking that she was a man. There was something even more insane about other people believing it.

Most insane was governments demanding that other people believe it. In May 2016, the Obama administration ordered American public schools to let students use whichever restrooms matched the gender with which they identified. From June 2016, the American military admitted the so-called transgendered.

The federal government was insane. Normal people knew it.

Trump reversed the gender insanity of the Obama era, at a federal level. President Biden resumed it.

Many conservatives are not Christian and many Christians are not conservative, but the more that conservatives and Christians held fast to sexual reality and morality when other Americans did not, the more Christianity and conservativism became synonymous in white people's minds, especially people considering themselves neither. Americans who had not considered themselves conservative found themselves called conservative because they recognized biological facts and norms that had been universally recognized only a decade or two earlier.

Immoral people criticized conservative Christians for supporting the twice divorced, allegedly adulterous, and generally boorish Trump. In October 2016, *The Washington Post* published a video recording from 2005 of Trump making lewd comments about women, as he and host Billy Bush were on their way to film an episode of the *Access Hollywood* television program. Trump publicly apologized for his words on that recording, as he rarely apologized for anything.

Publication of the recording promptly led to a spate of allegations from women that Trump had sexually assaulted or otherwise acted improperly towards them over the years. Trump denied the allegations.

In terms of policy, Trump was not legitimizing immorality. By apologizing for his recorded remarks and denying the allegations, he affirmed that lewd comments and sexual assault were immoral.

Women who had heard as much from other men, or knew that other men said as much, were generally not concerned about a private conversation between two men eleven years earlier. The timing of that release was blatantly an attempt to sway votes from Trump. Voters were similarly suspicious of allegations made against Trump amidst an election campaign, especially as regards a man in the public eye as Trump had been for years.

Like other Americans, Christian Americans choose candidates as best they can from those available, having regard to their values and interests. Their criteria are largely the same as other voters' criteria, along with regard to which candidates, whatever their faith or lack of it, will most likely in office defend Christianity.

Two thousand years have passed since a perfect person walked the earth. Christians do not expect any person walking the earth today to be perfect. "He that is without sin among you," said Christ, "let him cast the first stone..." Waiting for a perfect political candidate would be a luxury that democracy does not afford.

Whether Trump's sins were forgiven depended upon Trump. That was known only to God. Policies and practicalities mattered more than the character issues so important to Trump's critics.

In 2016, uncertain about Trump, Christians trusted other Christians. Conservatives trusted other conservatives.

Elected in 2012, Texas senator Ted Cruz was a longstanding conservative Christian, holding fast to his beliefs for which he was elected. Unafraid to criticize fellow Republicans in Congress, he had gusto aplenty.

An NBC television Survey Monkey poll released in January 2016 found the most common second choice for Trump voters was Cruz. The most common second choice for Cruz voters was Trump.

Cruz was loyal to his family, as conservatives and nationalists normally are. He blamed Trump for allegations in the *National Enquirer* newspaper in March 2016 that Cruz had committed adultery.

Conversely, and in spite of co-operation between political

campaigns and political action committees being illegal, Trump blamed the Cruz campaign for an image from a political action committee mocking Trump's wife Melania. *"Be careful, Lyin' Ted,"* tweeted Trump, *"or I will spill the beans on your wife!"*

As conservatives and nationalists normally do, Cruz remained kind about Trump's wife. *"Donald,"* Cruz tweeted, in response to a particularly nasty Trump tweet mocking Cruz' wife Heidi in March 2016, *"real men don't attack women. Your wife is lovely, and Heidi is the love of my life."*

In 1976, Ronald Reagan assured the Republican National Convention that he would vote for nominee Gerald Ford, without really endorsing Ford. Reagan used his speech to promote his beliefs.

In July 2016, Cruz could have done the same regarding Trump. He did not.

"After many months of careful consideration," said Cruz in a statement in September 2016, *"of prayer and searching my own conscience, I have decided that on Election Day, I will vote for the Republican nominee, Donald Trump."* He explained his decision in terms of policy. If Cruz could vote for Trump, so could other conservative Christians.

Another committed conservative Christian was Indiana governor Mike Pence. "I will be voting for Ted Cruz in the Republican primary," Pence told Greg Garrison of the WIBC radio station in April 2016. "I particularly want to commend Donald Trump, who I think has given voice to the frustration of millions of working Americans with a lack of progress in Washington, D.C."

Pence was everything that Trump was not. He was honest, calm, and measured. In 2002, Pence told *The Hill* newspaper that he never ate a meal with a woman not his wife and he did not attend events featuring alcohol without her by his side. Nobody accused Pence of adultery.

He was also a politician, with political skills to turn the votes of congressmen and women. After serving six terms in the House of Representatives before becoming Indiana governor, Pence understood the workings of Congress. He knew people there.

Trump selected Pence as his candidate for vice president, bringing Trump support from conservative Christians. Vice presidents being loyal to their presidents, they do not publicize disagreements between them.

Pence seemed never to compromise his conservatism or Christian faith. The Trump presidency drifted from Christian nationalism to Christian conservatism.

A free judiciary depends upon nationalism. Countries are founded upon nationalism. Their constitutions are premised upon nationalism.

Since World War II, Supreme Court judges had slowly stripped the American Constitution of the nationalism they no longer felt or might never have felt, at least for America. They played down the words of the Constitution in favor of what they claimed the Constitution implied, usurping authority from the American people, states, and legislatures. They stripped America of morality.

America introduced homosexual marriage not through an elected legislature or by popular vote. By a single-vote majority, the unelected Supreme Court in its 2013 decision in *United States v. Windsor* struck down the natural definition of marriage in the Defense of Marriage Act, 1996. Before 1996, there had been no need to define marriage, when marriage was universally known to be between man and woman.

The Fifth Amendment to the American Constitution had nothing to do with homosexuality, but the Supreme Court in 2013 interpreted Due Process to allow homosexual marriage. In 1791, when the Fifth Amendment was ratified, homosexuality was universally regarded as an abomination before man and God, to the extent that anyone thought of it.

Judicial leftists created law. Judicial conservatism became interpreting the law.

Whoever was elected president in 2016 would nominate a Supreme Court judge to replace the reliably conservative justice Antonin Scalia, who died early that year. Facing a Republican-controlled Senate, President Obama nominated to the court a legally qualified centrist Jew, who in earlier periods of American history the Senate would have confirmed. Reducing conservative judges by one, Obama thus sought to aid the leftist domination of the court.

As president, Obama had the right to nominate whomever he chose. The Senate had the right to affirm, reject, or not even consider that nomination. It had the duty to do so according to law and the well-being of the American people. The Senate could have refused to consider any non-conservative nominee in America's interests without the spurious reason of it being a presidential election year, although the Senate had been intermittently refusing to confirm judicial nominees in presidential election years since 1968.

Confident of winning the 2016 election, Democrats did not really object when the Senate refused to consider Obama's nominee. The coming President Hillary Clinton would nominate a leftist judge to the Supreme Court that the newly Democratic Senate would approve, cementing leftist control.

America no longer welcomed different voices. Leftists wanted their voices only.

Judicial appointments were a rare field in which Trump did not claim unrivalled expertise. He deferred to others presenting him with lists of names he did not recognize.

Many Americans had more pressing issues to worry about than court nominations, although court decisions could affect them. Those that could afford to care did because of one Supreme Court decision: *Roe v. Wade* in 1973, creating a Constitutional right to abortion.

Opposition to abortion rights was traditionally moral, although moral considerations could support abortion rights as a practical matter. Morality can be complex.

The Roman Catholic Church led American opposition to abortion, until President Reagan redefined American conservatism in the 1980s to oppose abortion rights. The issue became ideological: interpreting human life to whatever suited, preoccupied by rights, unconcerned with practicality or consequences upon people's lives.

Powerful people indulged conservatives with abortion restrictions upon other women. Rich women obtained safe abortions.

Many women through the late 1990s would have liked to vote Republican for the small, efficient, and responsible government as well as immigration, crime, taxation, and other policies, but they felt alienated by the Republican Party's rhetoric wanting to restrict their rights to abortion. Trump would have appealed to them. "I am pro-choice in every respect," he declared on *Meet the Press* in October 1999.

As they normally did, Trump's views changed over the years. He joined other Republican presidents since Reagan refusing to allow American foreign aid to fund abortions. Democrat presidents allowed it.

The separation between conservatism and nationalism was never more in evidence. Nationalists do not want money diverted from America's poor to aid other countries, but if money must go to other countries, then abortion and other birth control are the most useful expenditures to make.

Nationalist conservatives alleviate the reasons that compatriot women want abortions. If they restrict compatriot women's abortion rights, they care for mothers and children. They allow abortions of babies with Down's syndrome, if the mother wishes.

In 2017, Trump banned teenage illegal immigrants in federal custody from obtaining abortions. Conservatives were overjoyed. Nationalists saw no joy in a policy mandating anchor babies, who might someday demand American citizenship pursuant to the Fourteenth Amendment of the American Constitution.

The ban sparked a long legal battle. In 2020, Trump abandoned the ban.

By the end of Trump's presidency, with three new conservative judges appointed, Constitutionalists were back in the Supreme Court majority. In December 2020, the Court refused to hear Texas' lawsuit against four other states seeking to invalidate their 2020 presidential election results. No American law allowed one state to tell another state how to conduct elections.

"This is a great and disgraceful miscarriage of justice," tweeted Trump. *"The people of the United States were cheated, and our Country disgraced."* If Trump had expected his court nominees to do his bidding, delivering him a judicial coup d'état, then his claims of conservatism were a sham.

12. THE WUHAN VIRUS

The pandemic originating in China late in 2019 illustrated the necessity for nationalism: for Trump to have honored the promises he made in 2016. America needed to have reinvigorated her manufacturing to secure supply lines. She needed to have secured her borders and cut immigration.

Nationalism is a practical approach. Nationalists are practical people.

Outside the West, nationalism underpinned countries' responses to the pandemic. Globalism underpinned most Western responses, locking down citizens but generally leaving borders open. Individualism underpinned Trump's response.

Traditionally, officials often named viruses and diseases according to the places where they were first identified. Legionnaires' disease was first identified at a conference of the American Legion in 1976. The Ebola virus was first identified in two simultaneous outbreaks also in 1976, one in a village near the Ebola River in Congo.

Countries engaged in the Great War suppressed news of the influenza pandemic beginning in 1918, but with Spain out of the war, she reported her cases. The virus that eventually killed as many as a hundred million people became known as the Spanish 'flu, although it neither emanated from Spain nor particularly infected Spaniards. It might have emanated from China.

In 1968, the Hong Kong 'flu emanated from Hong Kong, killing from one to four million people worldwide. Unconfirmed reports traced it back to China.

From the outset, China suppressed news of a virus in Wuhan late in 2019. When news appeared, Western media spoke of the Wuhan virus, cluster, or outbreak. Only Chinese were victims.

With the West's globalist acquiescence, international bodies were becoming subject to Chinese dominion. *"Preliminary investigations conducted by the Chinese authorities have found no clear evidence of human-to-human transmission of the novel #coronavirus (2019-nCoV) identified in #Wuhan, #China,"* tweeted the World Health Organization in January 2020.

In mid-January 2020, Thailand reported the first case outside China. "Now we can say that it is certain that it is a human to human transmission phenomenon," admitted Chinese pulmonologist Zhong Nanshan a week later.

Two days after that, China appeared to prevent a World Health Organization meeting from warning the world about the severity of the virus. The Organization referred instead to *"divergent views."*

A day later, China quarantined Wuhan. Two days later, it locked down Hubei province. In the last week of January, China stopped all domestic airline flights from Hubei to the rest of China.

Chinese people spread their virus around the world, as did visitors to China returning home. No longer were Chinese the only victims. They were perpetrators of a pandemic, but white America does not treat other races as wrongdoers. Nor does she allow language that might connote something ill in other races. Calling it the Wuhan virus became racist.

Globalists are ideologues. They get angry about words.

When nationalists get angry about words, it is for their practical effect. Individualists can get angry about anything.

Enjoying the power the West gave it, China prohibited the world from using language that might diminish its prestige. In 2015, the World Health Organization formulated new practices for naming diseases, avoiding place names. In February 2020, the Organization named the Wuhan virus the coronavirus disease of 2019, abbreviated to COVID-19.

The American Legion did not object to Legionnaires' disease being so named. Spain and Hong Kong did not object to the names of those viruses. Villagers near the Ebola River did not object to the name of that virus. They were not building an empire.

"We have waged a fierce battle against the invisible enemy: The China virus," said Trump, addressing the United Nations in a recorded speech in September 2020. "As we pursue this bright future, we must hold accountable the nation which unleashed this plague onto the world: China. The United Nations must hold China accountable for their actions." Neither Trump nor the United Nations did.

"In addition to inflaming racism," wrote University of Pittsburgh assistant professor of history Mari Webel in March 2020,

"emphasizing the foreign or external origins of a disease influences how people understand their own risk of disease and whether they change their behavior."

Defending globalism and diversity, Americans insisted the virus could have arisen anywhere, but if the virus came from bats, then it could only have arisen among people eating bats, using bats in traditional medicine, or buying bats from wet markets. If the virus came from the Wuhan viral laboratories, then Chinese safeguards were inadequate. Among the lies coming from China, the virus' origins remained unclear.

While Americans diverted blame from China, China diverted blame towards America. In March 2020, the *Global Times* newspaper, an organ of the Chinese Communist Party, suggested that an American military cyclist attending the Military World Games in Wuhan in October 2019 might have brought the virus from Fort Detrick, Maryland. Zhao Lijian, the deputy director general of the Information Department of China's Foreign Ministry, speculated in a tweet that America had concealed initial virus deaths in 'flu data.

America only blames white people. In August 2020, New York governor Andrew Cuomo spoke of the European virus because a strain of the virus came to America from Europe, without acknowledging that the virus came to Europe from China.

In January 2021, the mutation of the virus first detected in the United Kingdom was the U.K. strain. The mutation first detected in Brazil was the Brazilian strain.

Nobody objected to those names. Globalists only erase local descriptors when it suits.

The place quickest to respond to the first reports of a virus in Wuhan with measures to protect its people was Taiwan, early in January 2020. It did not trust the government in Beijing.

The West, including Trump, trusted the government in Beijing. The West trusts other races, mistrusting only white people. Any fear of catching the virus from Wuhan was another phobia to malign white people maligned with no end of politically driven phobias. It was racism.

When a Chinese couple visiting Rome tested positive for the virus late in January 2020, the Italian government banned airplane flights from China. Appalled at the Italian government's racism, *"The mayor of Florence, Italy, @DarioNardella initiated "hug a Chinese" on Twitter on Feb 1,"* tweeted the *Global Times* newspaper, with pictures, *"opposing anger toward China amid the #nCoV2019 outbreak, and calling for "Unity in this common battle!" Many Italian netizens responded by posting photos of themselves with Chinese."*

Better dead than racist, passers-by in Milan and Florence hugged Chinese holding placards inviting Italians to hug them. Italy had sold much of her fashion industry to China years earlier and admitted thousands of Chinese to work in it, shuffling back and forth between China and Italy. That was globalism.

Dismissing the virus, American House of Representatives speaker Nancy Pelosi toured San Francisco's Chinatown in February 2020. Calling upon visitors to come, she insisted "everything is fine here."

Chinese restaurants in Australia suffered reduced patronage. People presumed that was more white racism, but it was Chinese people fearing the virus staying away, not Australians cheerfully unaware of the danger. Always shouldering the white man's burden to help other races, Australians were supposed to dine more in Chinese restaurants to aid those restauranteurs and staff, while Chinese stayed safely away.

From the beginning of February 2020, Australia banned travel from China, but lives are one thing. Money matters more, for the individualist West.

The University of Western Sydney offered to pay fifteen hundred dollars towards the costs of its Chinese students coming to Australia via other countries. Melbourne University offered its Chinese students seven and a half thousand dollars to spend to circumvent the ban.

In the middle of March, over a cascading few days, the West turned to fear. None of the prior pandemics through history so frightened people, at least since the Black Death, but by 2020, the West had become estranged from death. Its specter had become too much to bear.

European countries closed borders between countries that had been open for decades, keeping out fellow Europeans however well they were. Borders remained open to asylum seekers and other immigrants from outside the West, whatever diseases they carried.

Globalism was never more obviously fatal. Nationalism never more obviously saves people.

With nationalism rare in the West, Australia and New Zealand allowed only their citizens and residents along with their partners and families to enter each country from March 2020. Arrivals were subject to fourteen-day quarantine.

Constrained by the capacity of quarantine hotels to accommodate returnees, Australia from March 2020 banned her citizens from leaving the country except with permission, pursuant to the Biosecurity Act. Only a third of applicants in 2020 obtained permission to leave.

Australia also closed borders within the country that had been open for a century and borders that had always been open. All Australian states closed at least one border at some point during 2020, as did the Northern Territory. The Australian Capital Territory restricted admissions. People permitted to enter each jurisdiction included residents returning home, normally then quarantined from the rest of the population for fourteen days.

Some arrivals quarantined at home. Others quarantined in hotels.

Queensland remained largely virus free, until Olivia Winnie Muranga, Diana Lasu, and Haja Umu Timbo returned from interstate travel in July and lied about having been in virus-affected Victoria. They had flown to Melbourne to join other Africans stealing handbags, among the African crime gangs that Victorian police once denied existed, before downplaying.

With her borders closed more tightly, Western Australia was also virus-free when African women Banchi Techana and Isata Jalloh flew into Perth from Adelaide in August for a party. Without a return flight available, they were ordered into quarantine in the Novotel hotel, but hotel security guards could not keep them from leaving the hotel to attend the party. When police telephoned one of the women to order her back to quarantine, she laughed and hung up the telephone.

Ordered to leave the state, Jalloh told media she would return and "enter by force." Australia had welcomed her as a refugee.

In December 2020, Western Australia allowed Jalloh to return to attend a funeral. Supposedly quarantined for two weeks in a Northbridge hotel, she hosted guests and repeatedly left, shopping for liquor for a party. There was no funeral.

Indigenous Australians were no more co-operative. While the rest of the Sydney Swans football team quarantined in the Joondalup Resort in Perth, also in August, indigenous player Elijah Taylor's indigenous girlfriend Lekahni Pearce snuck in to meet him. A month later, unrelated to that, police would charge Taylor with assaulting her.

Western governments trying to slow the spread of the virus imposed restrictions upon people within their jurisdictions, unprecedented in peacetime or wartime. They shut people in their homes upon conditions, restricted their movements outside, and capped the numbers attending public and private gatherings.

White people and East Asians largely followed the rules, recommendations, and restrictions. Police fined people breaching the law, in parks and in cars. They arrested people in their homes, including pregnant Zoe Buhler, posting messages on social media supporting protests against the restrictions.

Rarely paying attention to other races misbehaving, officials noticing recalcitrant races knew better than to mention it. When the Victorian chief health officer Brett Sutton in September 2020 mentioned Afghans breaching the rules, he subsequently apologized to the Afghan community for what he called "inadvertently" singling them out.

For the sake of community relations, Western police prefer not to arrest people of other races. In the spirit of inclusion, Western governments might as well exempt them and their religions from restrictions they were not following anyway. The New South Wales government restricted religious services generally, while granting an exemption to the Auburn Gallipoli mosque for four hundred Muslims celebrating Eid al-Adha in August 2020.

Clusters arose among immigrant races because immigrants congregate in communities. White people are individuals.

Clusters arose among white people because infected people of other races felt no moral deterrent from infecting races not their own. Governments did not identify people illegally working while awaiting virus test results or while knowing they were infected with the virus, earning money they would have otherwise not earned. Most significant were the aged-care workers, such as one ultimately killing nineteen people at the Newmarch House nursing home in Sydney. In better times, aged-care workers had been particular favorites of governments lauding immigrants filling jobs.

Speaking to *Unherd* in April 2020, Swedish epidemiologist Johan Giesecke suggested that Sweden failed to protect her elderly in nursing homes from the virus because asylum seekers and refugees on staff "may not always be understanding the information," as if immigrants could not otherwise have known of the pandemic or restrictions. World wars had not consumed world news and public attention as had the pandemic and restrictions of 2020.

There was a view that Sweden knew immigrants would not comply with restrictions, so imposed fewer restrictions than other Western countries in response to the pandemic. If so, Sweden's leaders let the virus spread and Swedes die rather than admit immigrant lawlessness.

Sweden's response was much like the response that Trump wanted for America. She imposed restrictions upon large gatherings and upon people entering nursing homes, but without locking the population down as other European countries did.

Trump's problem was the impression that his motivation was not the American people but the American economy and his re-election effort. Sweden's leaders invoked the calm assurance that they were acting for Swedes' well-being, as economic activity can be, to a point. They presented experts who supported them.

That did not make Sweden's response right. It simply made it more credible at the time than it seemed coming from Trump.

In December 2020 and January 2021, Sweden tightened her restrictions and increased their enforcement. The economic impact of the pandemic was less in Sweden than it was in neighboring countries, but the deaths thus far were much worse. Only at the end of the pandemic might a judgement be possible.

When masks were not mandatory in Sydney, the only people obviously wearing them were East Asians. Having become used to wearing them in their homelands through past epidemics, they were protecting themselves and each other.

The Victorian government told a parliamentary inquiry established in October 2020 into its contact tracing system that the foreign born comprised thirty percent of the state's population and half the virus cases. Twenty-nine percent of cases spoke a language other than English at home. In August 2020, the Victorian government dedicated twenty-five million dollars for additional support services dedicated to immigrants.

In America, the Centers for Disease Control and Prevention published data to the end of November 2020 suggesting greater infection, hospitalization, and mortality rates among minority races than white people, other than infection rates among Asians, which were lower. The differences with Asians were small, but the differences with other races were significant, with their mortality rates approaching three times that for white people.

Americans did not imagine those other races breaching rules related to the virus any more than they imagined other races committing other wrongdoing. Nor did Americans dwell upon obesity or other factors affecting health and morbidity, which correlated with race. Instead, Americans blamed structural racism: the racism that white people do not think, feel, or practice.

Conversely, government responses were systemic racism favoring other races. In December 2020, at least eighteen American states prioritized minority races over white Americans in getting the vaccine that would soon become available, in accordance with the Centers for Disease Control's social vulnerability index. Minority races were more reluctant than white people to take vaccinations.

The elderly were most vulnerable to the virus, but University of Pennsylvania ethics professor Harald Schmidt wanted workers favored for the vaccine because workers were more likely to be from racial minorities. "Older populations are whiter," he told *The New York Times* newspaper. "Society is structured in a way that enables them to live longer. Instead of giving additional health benefits to those who already had more of them, we can start to level the playing field a bit." In the name of equality, white people could die.

Never do people need nationalism more than when facing a common threat, whether human, viral, or anything else. Never are the failings of globalism and individualism more in evidence than in white people's refusal to face that threat together. Never is the damage of diversity more devastating.

Racially homogenous Japan, Korea, and Vietnam experienced the pandemic, but their people followed rules that minimized infections and deaths. They suffered less economically than America did.

Racial homogeneity did not save some countries. Races differ.

Singapore initially fared well through the pandemic because its dominant Chinese population complied with its rules, while the virus lingered among South Asian migrant workers crammed together. The virus reared again in April 2020.

A plausible hypothesis for anyone willing to consider issues of race rationally is that the pandemic would have killed fewer people, inflicted less economic harm, and required fewer restrictions upon Western countries were Western cities still homogenous. Western governments and news media worried less about other races spreading a lethal virus than about white people responding with racism.

They need not have worried. As of March 2021, the Wuhan virus had killed more than two million people worldwide, including more Americans and Italians than Chinese. It had infected more than a hundred million people and ruined economies. Still, the West refused to be racist.

Trump's chance to secure America had passed. China's leaders remained in power, exploiting the opportunities the pandemic presented to advance China towards superpower status, dislodging America.

America complied. Within a week after taking office, President Biden issued an executive order banning American federal agencies and public health documents and resources from referring to the China virus or Wuhan virus. Never more plainly was America consumed with death by diversity.

13. COMPASSION

The essence of nationalism is people caring for their compatriots. The essence of individualism is people caring for themselves. The essence of globalism is supposed to be people caring for everyone, but it always ends up with people caring only for themselves.

Nationalism inspires compassion for one's compatriots. Individualism and globalism lead to compassion for no one.

Trump *"doesn't understand his own base,"* wrote conservative columnist Peggy Noonan in June 2020. She could have said it in many respects.

In October 2020, Trump tweeted an image of an old people's home with the Democrat nominee Joe Biden campaign logo and the P struck through in the word *"President,"* to say Biden was fit only to be resident in an old people's home. Did Trump think the same of senior voters?

Biden could confuse his words, as everybody does and for which Republicans were routinely mocked while Democrats were generally not. It did not matter.

It might have helped Biden. It made him seem natural, unrehearsed and honest, much as Trump's abuse had done for him four years earlier. Lying can require a sharp mind. Trump's mind was sharp.

No conservative political candidate was doing more to alienate his or her normally strong support among the elderly since British prime minister Theresa May's proposed so-called dementia tax in her snap 2017 election campaign. May learnt, hurriedly killed that proposal, but never recovered.

Trump never seemed to learn. Learning would admit he had previously been wrong.

In the case of Biden, Trump mocked a senior white male Christian, and thus from the demographic that was Trump's deepest support. In the case of longstanding Arizona senator John McCain, Trump attacked a senior white male Christian and war veteran, and thus from two demographics that were Trump's deepest support.

Nations require defense. American soldiers, sailors, and airmen understood as much when they went to war in America's defense, many sacrificing their lives.

Trump's nationalism never went so far. Neither did Clinton, Obama, or Biden serve in America's military. As much a function of the time in which he lived, the last president to see active military duty was George H W Bush.

During the Vietnam War, McCain was held prisoner in North Vietnam for five and a half years, during which time he was tortured. "He was captured," Trump said to Dan Rather of *CBS News* in January 2000, in a wide-ranging discussion of a possible future run for president. "Does being captured make you a hero? I don't know. I'm not sure."

Patriotic Americans do not mock prisoners of war. They especially do not mock American prisoners of war.

In 2008, McCain was the Republican Party nominee for president. Losing to Obama, he thus remained a senator from Arizona, as he had been since 1987.

Trump had reasons to disagree with McCain on policy. Chairman of the Senate Armed Services Committee, McCain personified the globalist attitude that searched for wars around the world to join. When the Syrian Civil War erupted in March 2011, McCain initially hesitated. "I don't see a way that we could intervene militarily," he told France-24 television in April 2011.

At the time, McCain was advocating bombing Libya. That happened.

"Now that military operations in Libya are ending," McCain told a meeting of the World Economic Forum in Jordan in October 2011, "there will be renewed focus on what partial military operations might be considered to protect civilian lives in Syria."

By May 2014, McCain wanted American military intervention against the Syrian government. "All of us, Americans and Europeans," he told the European Union – Washington Forum at the Fairfax Hotel, Washington in May 2014, "must recognize that our power infers a responsibility on us."

In June 2015, McCain said he disagreed with Trump's comments about Mexicans in America. It set off an increasingly personal exchange of criticisms from both men, with little talk of policy.

As was often the case with Trump, his opinion of McCain varied widely. "You know, frankly," he told radio host Don Imus in May 2016, "I like John McCain, and John McCain is a hero." Those comments were not the comments people remembered.

In July 2017, McCain's brain tumor became public. At the end of that month, McCain and other senators thwarted Trump's efforts to honor at least in part Trump's campaign promise to repeal the Affordable Care Act, after more extensive repeal bids failed in Congress.

McCain's strange reason was that the repeal did not go far enough. *"From the beginning, I have believed that Obamacare should be repealed and replaced with a solution that increases competition, lowers costs, and improves care for the American people,"* said McCain in a statement afterwards. *"The so-called 'skinny repeal' amendment the Senate voted on today would not accomplish those goals."* McCain's renown was for being a maverick.

As an individualist would, Trump seemed to see everything in terms of personal battles and relationships. After McCain voted against another attempt in the Senate to repeal parts of the Affordable Care Act in September 2017, known as the Graham–Cassidy legislation sponsored by South Carolina senator Lindsey Graham, Trump tweeted: *"McCain let his best friend L.G. down!"*

Graham had been a vocal Never-Trump Republican before the 2016 election, before becoming an enthusiastic supporter through the years. Graham's response to Trump's tweet was that of a nationalist. *"My friendship with @SenJohnMcCain is not based on how he votes,"* said Graham in a statement, *"but respect for how he's lived his life and the person he is."*

Trump continued attacking the terminally ill McCain. "We had a gentleman way into the morning hours, go thumbs-down," Trump told a rally in Duluth, Minnesota in June 2018. "He went thumbs-down."

McCain died in August 2018. McCain's family let it be known that McCain had not wanted Trump at his funeral. Trump did not attend.

In April 2018, McCain had published his memoir *The Restless Wave*, in which he expressed his regret at not having selected his friend Senator Joe Lieberman as his running mate in 2008. Instead, he chose Alaska governor Sarah Palin, who McCain's widow also declined to invite to his funeral.

Palin responded as a nationalist. *"Out of respect to Senator McCain and his family,"* journalist Kelly O'Donnell quoted a Palin family source in a tweet, *"we have nothing to add at this point. The Palin family will always cherish their friendship with the McCains and hold those memories dear."*

The nationalism that keeps out of other people's wars also honored McCain for having fought on America's behalf, however long ago that was. For his war record, public service, and family at least, American nationalists respected and honored McCain. Nationalists leave policy differences behind when compatriots near death and die.

Trump won the state of Arizona in 2016, when Arizona had two Republican senators, including McCain. Trump lost the state in 2020, after which Arizona had no Republican senators.

Might Trump have been re-elected in 2020 if he had respected McCain? He certainly would have polled better in Arizona, which had voted for Republican candidates for president in every election since 1996.

Responding to the Wuhan Virus

Nationalism recognizes the benefit that compatriots' lives are to each other. Nationalism wants to keep them healthy and alive.

When a crisis strikes a country, elected officials need to be seen to care for the people. If they care, they need to display their care.

If they do not care, they need to pretend to care, with words of sympathy and support. Leaders need to be seen to be nationalist, with all the compassion for their people that nationalism commands.

In February 2020, Trump's campaign manager Brad Parscale was on the telephone with Trump and senior White House officials when someone asked Parscale what worried him the most. He said the virus, reported *Politico* in November 2020.

"This ... virus," snapped Trump, according to a person with direct knowledge of the conversation, "what does it have to do with me getting re-elected?"

Many a politician has been re-elected without demonstrating any compassion, at least for Americans. Those politicians were not re-elected during a pandemic.

Had Trump revived American manufacturing and secured her borders, then America would have been better placed to face the pandemic taking hold of the planet. Instead, the pandemic accentuated his shortcomings.

Public health systems and centers for disease control around the world were unprepared for a pandemic, especially those systems and centers politicized for years on pointless political and social programs. Without nationalism uniting people, everything in America was politicized.

Nevertheless, the pandemic could have guaranteed Trump's re-election, had he handled it well in the circumstances. What could be more American First than saving American lives?

Other leaders and governments around the world were rewarded by their electorates for seeming to respond well. Among those governments were those in New Zealand and the Australian states and territories with elections that year. Those governments sealed their national and state borders, as America and other Western countries did not.

Were it not for the pandemic, Trump might well have been re-elected in 2020, but the pandemic did not cost Trump re-election. His response to it might have done.

Pollster Tony Fabrizio, of the firm Fabrizio, Lee & Associates, examined Trump's loss in his December 2020 report *Post Election Exit Poll Analysis: 10 Key Target States*. "*Coronavirus (CV) was the top issue…,*" Fabrizio concluded, "*and Biden carried those voters nearly 3 to 1.*"

At his best, Trump was a nationalist. From the end of January 2020, Trump banned people without American citizenship or permanent residency who had been in China within the previous fourteen days from flying from China to America, unless they had immediate family members who were American citizens or permanent residents.

As always, Trump subordinated nationalism to business interests. Exceptions to the ban allowed American citizens and permanent residents to continue flying back and forth between America and China.

In mid-March 2020, Trump announced fifteen days of guidelines to slow the spread of the virus, which he later extended to the end of April. He encouraged Americans to remain at least six feet apart from each other and to work from home. They should avoid restaurants, gatherings of ten or more people, and discretionary travel. He advised older Americans and those with serious underlying health conditions to isolate themselves. "Our country wasn't built to be shut down," he told a media briefing late in March 2020.

Trump's narcissism was never more evident than with his daily media briefings, beginning mid-March 2020. Instead of informing Americans about the pandemic and Washington's response, they conveyed the sense of Trump promoting himself. Trump made the virus about him.

With a new virus, there was always going to be a range of expert medical opinion. Public opinion of potential treatments depended upon people's support for Trump trying to promote optimism or their opposition to him generally.

In response to criticism, Trump did not change the briefings. He suspended them, in April 2020. Trump's erratic behavior stopped being a curiosity to become a worry when it played over into his incoherent ramshackle response to the virus. Briefings did not resume until July.

Trump's guidelines wound up at the end of April 2020. "They'll be fading out because now the governors are doing it," Trump told reporters in the Oval Office. "I don't want people to get used to this… I see the new normal being what it was three months ago."

In normal times, voters prefer optimism to pessimism. These were not normal times.

Nothing better demonstrated Western individualism than disregarding American lives, rich or poor, to keep the economy going. Trump had been elected in 2016 because past presidents had prioritized economic indices above Americans' well-being, which downgraded American lives during healthy times. It downgraded them even more during a pandemic.

For nationalists, economies are only important for the benefits they provide people, as was a message of Trump's 2016 campaign. The dead care nothing for gross domestic product.

Life and economic well-being could be balanced. Especially for small businesses and people dependent upon them, they had to be balanced.

Trump's businesses were big. His response to the pandemic brought into sharp relief concerns that he was too close to big commercial interests instead of the people.

It also exacerbated other concerns about him: that he preferred to talk, tweet, and play golf than work; that he was preoccupied with himself and his re-election, without understanding that the best course for his re-election was to handle the pandemic well. Telling people to behave without thought of the pandemic for the sake of the economy translated to telling people they could become sick and die to aid his re-election effort.

In short, it highlighted the limits to Trump's nationalism: that it was not nationalism at all. Trump misjudged badly to think that dismissing the virus to keep the economy sailing through would re-elect him. In the choice between economies and health, Americans choose health. There did not need to be a choice, but it seemed as if there was.

Individualism was never more self-destructive than it was when Americans refused in the name of liberty to take relatively simple health precautions. Where is the liberty in getting sick and dying?

Within countries and in preparation for travel to some other countries, medical advice had long been for people to take particular vaccines. While opponents cited claims of health problems, underlying those claims was their objection to vaccinations being pressured upon people, even forced upon them. It was the zealous individualism that refuses any intrusion upon a person's life, even if that intrusion saves that person's life or other people's lives.

Compounding their objections was a deep mistrust of government and big corporations. Governments and big corporations brought that about.

Recommendations are not requirements in free societies. Individualism refuses the intrusion of even recommendations.

This was the era in which people placed stickers on their motorcars expressing their abuse of cancer, as if cancer could be abused into erasure. Increasingly, Trump responded to the pandemic the same way.

Trump could have valued American lives by supporting expert medical advice with no adverse economic impact. Could not all church services have been conducted through television and computers, as became the norm in Sydney?

That advice could change with new data and other information. In April 2020, Trump announced that the Centers for Disease Control and Prevention recommended wearing a face mask. There would have been no harm in Trump supporting that recommendation as a precaution, especially in confined places. Masks comforted people, not just to wear but to see on others. Instead, Trump stressed that "you do not have to do it."

Trump generally did not wear a mask, seeming to treat it as a form of weakness and submission. At a White House briefing in September 2020, he mocked Biden wearing one. "Maybe he doesn't want to expose his face," said Trump.

Wearing a mask became perceived as opposition to Trump. Not wearing a mask declared confidence in Trump: in individualism.

In a country that respects private property, shopkeepers and others should be free to set whatever rules they wish upon people wanting to enter their premises or remain there. They should have the right to exclude people not wearing masks, if they wish.

People caring about others not wearing masks where mask wearing was mandatory, or not wearing their masks correctly, advise them of their error. Nationalism makes people welcome other people caring enough about them to mention it.

Amidst rampant individualism, such care became an intrusion upon people's lives like fascism or communism, as if fascism and communism were simply matters of mask wearing. "*Who elected you mask monitor?*" was the substance of the social media response, even if that was not the response in person. It became simpler and easier to say nothing, even if that meant letting someone get sick and die.

Trump resumed his rallies in June 2020, gathering strangers together in communicable range, most without masks. It was the worst of Trump, risking people's lives for the sake not of economic activity, but of him and his re-election bid.

Nobody had to attend the rallies, but people did. Anybody infected there could return home afterwards and infect people not there. They might infect their families. They might infect strangers in a store. To voters already concerned that Trump had failed to respond responsibly to the virus, the rallies reinforced the realization that he was fundamentally irresponsible and foolhardy.

Unable to keep himself from becoming infected in October 2020 affirmed Trump's failure to protect America. That he was so bullish in recovery might have added to the Superman image he thought that he projected, but it also added to the space between him and mortal Americans worried about falling sick and dying.

Biden's public speeches were not rallies. They were lackluster affairs before small audiences spaced around open air. They suited a lackluster candidate offering a calmer presidency than Trump's presidency had been.

Americans were not looking for excitement or defiance. They were looking to stay alive.

Biden's gatherings expressed a sense that he was treating the pandemic seriously. Nobody would become infected. Nobody would go home and infect others. That he was so responsible a candidate suggested that he would be as responsible a president, conveying a reassuring promise of competence.

Thus Biden exuded more nationalism than Trump exuded. Nationalism need not be loud or raucous. It can be soft and gentle.

Nationalism does not need a crowd. It is simply a nation: governments aiding the people and people aiding each other. Amidst a pandemic still at its peak, or worse still not yet at its peak, nationalism needed to be distant, more distant than individualism.

14. OTHER PEOPLE'S NATIONALISM

For races other than white people, racism remains normal. Thus nationalism remains normal. Their races are their nations, or several nations.

Aside from Eastern Europe, white people avert racial tensions by submitting to other races. When white people refuse to submit, racial tensions resurface. People thus blame white people for those tensions.

When white people harm someone from another race, even in defending their lives or property, other white people are appalled. Victims from other races need not forgive white people, even innocent white people, as white people forgive wrongdoers of other races.

White people allow other races their hatred and vengeance towards them, which they would refuse to allow towards other races. They share their hatred and vengeance too. America calls it social justice, although it is neither social nor justice.

Americans do not protest the deaths of white people by black, white, or other American police officers as they protest the deaths of black people, even criminals resisting arrest and dying for no fault of the police. Unconcerned with the thousands more black people killed each year by other black people, black nationalism inspired the Black Lives Matter movement in 2013.

The wealthy white populace unable to believe that black people could be criminals, or be criminals at a greater rate than white people, took aim at itself, certain that white people were innately racist and white society institutionally racist, but that other people and societies were not. White people taking responsibility for black people's actions meant that black people did not need to take responsibility.

Anti-racist white Americans abused black police, treating black police as collaborators with their white society they abhorred. Black Lives Matter was a movement against white people and societies.

When facing a risk of death, police officers were supposed to be willing to die rather than defend themselves, if defending themselves harmed black people. They could kill white people, but not black people.

For refusing to submit to black nationalism, declaring that all lives matter or that white lives matter became racist. All lives did not matter. White lives did not matter.

Black Lives Matter was more than black nationalism. It was black supremacy.

In April 2017, *The New York Times* newspaper reported that Jared Kushner was pressing Trump to reduce criminal sentencing across America, so as to entice black voters towards Trump; criminals were disproportionately black. Kushner faced resistance from Attorney General Jeff Sessions, who wanted tougher criminal sentencing.

Kushner prevailed. In December 2018, Trump signed the Formerly Incarcerated Re-enter Society Transformed Safely Transitioning Every Person Act, later known by its acronym the First Step Act. It amended federal criminal sentencing laws to reduce the number of people in prisons and supposedly reduce recidivism.

Nationalism protects people from crime. If the First Step Act served America's national interest, it was not obvious.

Was Trump only seeking black votes, or did he promote the First Step Act to sign something dramatic into law after signing so little dramatic into law, other than tax cuts? If bombing Syria made Trump like any other president while cutting taxes and restricting abortion made him like any other Republican, then sparing criminals from jail made him like any Democrat.

In Congress, the First Step Act enjoyed bipartisan support. That Republicans followed Trump's lead suggested much about Trump's influence over Congressional Republicans, which he did not utilize to cut immigration.

Had Hillary Clinton been elected president in 2016 and passed the First Step Act during her time in office, then Republicans probably would have opposed it. Trump would almost certainly have tweeted his condemnation of her being lax on crime: inviting people to be criminal, freeing criminals from jail to be criminal again.

When Black Lives Matter riots seized American cities in May 2020, citizen Trump might well have tweeted his blame upon the hypothetical President Hillary Clinton and the First Step Act for the riots, although the Act had no obvious role. The riots followed a smartphone recording of the police arrest for passing counterfeit money in Minneapolis of George Floyd, a black man six feet and four inches tall weighing more than two hundred and twenty pounds, who had been convicted in 2007 of armed robbery in a home invasion. Floyd died.

With President Trump, the First Step Act remained unmentioned. There were no such tweets from Democrats for a law that Democrats wanted or from Republicans for a law that Republicans passed.

Democrats blamed police for the 2020 riots. Confident in the kindness of black people, activists called for defunding the police, replacing them with social workers and services.

Republicans blamed Democrats in office in those cities. Nobody blamed black people or questioned racial diversity.

Trump spoke with Floyd's family, before a gathering with industry leaders late in May 2020. "I think that it's sad in so many ways from the standpoint of the family," Trump told journalists. "When you look at George Floyd and his family and you see what that's done to them, just a terrible thing. He was in tremendous pain obviously, and couldn't breathe. It was a very, very sad thing for me to see that."

Police responded to the riots as America responded. Many knelt down, bending their knees in submission to the rioters. Others resigned from their force.

The violence was a small sense of civil war, but America was familiar with civil war. Minnesota governor Tim Walz summoned the National Guard to quell the violence.

Trump offered to send the American military to assist. *"Any difficulty and we will assume control but,"* tweeted Trump near the end of May 2020, *"when the looting starts, the shooting starts."*

Three decades earlier, in 1989, the Chinese government set Chinese troops against peaceful civilian pro-democracy protestors in Tiananmen Square, Beijing, killing hundreds. To Western eyes, sending troops against its citizens demonstrated the wickedness of the communist regime.

To Chinese eyes like Zhenya (known also as Dio) Wang, later a Western Australian senator in the Australian parliament, the Chinese government acted properly. "Based on the information I have," he told the *Australian Financial Review* in June 2015, "I think the government did the right thing."

With Chinese nationalism was Chinese supremacy. A few days later, Wang supported Chinese territorial claims in the South China Sea.

Protests are one thing. Crimes are another.

Unlike the protests in Tiananmen Square thirty-one years earlier, the rioting in America in 2020 was violent and destructive, but Trump's defense secretary Mark Esper opposed the use of military force on American streets. Before his appointment in July 2019, Esper had been a lobbyist for defense contractors.

Soon after the 2020 election, Trump fired Esper. Trump firing his appointees could only have helped them in their rehabilitation with the rest of Washington.

Black Lives Matter protests were not confined to America. Across the West, white people were certain that black people were victims of white prejudice.

Governments that prohibited public gatherings for health reasons nevertheless permitted Black Lives Matter protests for political reasons. Not even a pandemic kept white people from supporting black people.

In Australia, black people were primarily indigenous Aborigines. In Britain, they were free immigrants and their children and grandchildren.

Joining other Britons on British streets, British police meekly descended on bended knee, in submission to immigrants they were not arresting anyway. British police preferred to arrest white people, if only for racism.

British police thus invited immigrant races to treat them with ever more contempt. Early in June 2020, a smartphone recorded a black man assaulting a white policeman patrolling a footpath in daylight along Frampton Park Road, Hackney, north London, wrestling the policeman to the ground. Several black men and a black boy rushed in, three of them beating or kicking the solitary white policeman. Another black man danced around recording himself on his smartphone at the scene. The policeman writhed in self-protection, fending off the attacks as best he could, but he dared not harm his assailants. White bystanders pulled away.

From elsewhere along Frampton Park Road, a black policewoman hurried in. Without the white policeman's fear, she pushed the assailants away. There were no riots in response.

In America, the riots continued. Trump's focus was himself.

"My Admin has done more for the Black Community than any President since Abraham Lincoln," Trump tweeted in June 2020. *"Passed Opportunity Zones with @SenatorTimScott, guaranteed funding for HBCU's, School Choice, passed Criminal Justice Reform, lowest Black unemployment, poverty, and crime rates in history."*

Opportunity Zones facilitated investments in poor areas. An H.B.C.U. was a historically black college or university. School Choice widened parents' choices concerning public schools for their children.

While other politicians rushed to side ever more with black nationalism, Trump was more circumspect during an interview with Catherine Herridge of *CBS News* in July 2020. "Why are African Americans still dying at the hands of law enforcement in this country?" she asked him.

"And so are white people," replied Trump. "So are white people. What a terrible question to ask? So are white people. More white people, by the way, more white people."

Such rational nationalistic moments earned Trump his electoral support in 2016 and maintained most of it through his time in office. They defended his race, without harming other races. Substantive actions rarely accompanied his words.

The persistent riots around America were opportunities for others to join. Owing their origins to the 1920s and '30s, Antifa groups opposed not just fascism, as most Americans did, but also white people and society they considered innately and institutionally fascist, almost by definition.

Antifa could be as nationalist as anyone, but it was black, Muslim, or any other nationalism but white or Christian. They might not have considered themselves Marxist, but their ideological origins lay with Marx. If modern-day Marxists knew what Karl Marx believed about race, they would either not be Marxists or they would not be supporting black nationalism.

That Antifa groups were often middle-class white people said much about the failure of individualism. People of other races had their races and nations, their racism and nationalism, while white people sought new groups to join. Among their options was Antifa: the anti-nationalist nationalism.

They might have looted stores to take whatever their parents did not buy them. They might have assailed police and society too much like their distant parents, or because their parents assailed police and society too.

The Saxons of Saxony were reputedly the best of Nazis under Nazism. When the Soviet Union imposed communism on eastern Germany, they became the best of communists.

What might modern-day Antifa groups become if they could be weaned from Antifa? What might they achieve if they could turn Antifa hatred into patriotic love, turn the destruction of Marxism into the construction of nationalism?

No less reflecting the failure of individualism than the Antifa groups were the Proud Boys, founded in 2016 and led in 2020 by mixed-race Enrique Tarrio. They, not the police, were the best known protectors of Americans and Americans' property in the face of black and Antifa violence in 2020.

"Proud Boys," said Trump, during his first presidential debate with Democrat nominee Joe Biden in Cleveland near the end of September 2020, "stand back and stand by."

"President Trump told the proud boys to stand by because someone needs to deal with ANTIFA," responded Proud Boys member Joe Biggs on Parler social media, *"well sir! we're ready!!"*

Nationalists stand together. Individualists stand alone.

In response to criticism of his comment, Trump wilted. "I condemn all white supremacists," he told *Fox News* at the start of October 2020. The West's support of other races' advancing nationalism and supremacy did not lead to tolerance of any lingering white nationalism or supremacy. "I condemn the Proud Boys. I don't know much about the Proud Boys, but I condemn that."

Trump's few interests through December 2020 included his response to a defense-spending bill, which included renaming American military bases named for Confederate figures, in submission to black nationalism. It was a measure of Trump's failure.

By then, not even killing more than six hundred thousand white people in the American Civil War was enough for President Lincoln to have proven that black lives mattered enough for him. "Lincoln," said Jeremiah Jeffries, the chairman of the School Names Advisory Committee for the San Francisco Unified School District, in December 2020, "like the presidents before him and most after, did not show through policy or rhetoric that black lives ever mattered to them outside of human capital and as casualties of wealth building."

In their shared conflict with white America, black lives had effectively become any lives but white lives. The Committee put Lincoln High School on its list for consideration of name changing because of Lincoln's treatment of Native Americans.

Jeffries was a first-grade teacher. He was black.

Lincoln was one of forty-four San Francisco schools to be renamed. In February 2021, the school board suspended the process to focus on reopening schools closed with the pandemic.

A particularly spectacular list of black nationalist demands was laid upon the elite Dalton School in New York in December 2020. Those demands included paying the student debt of black staffers upon hiring them, hiring twelve full-time diversity officers, and hiring multiple psychologists to support students *"coping with race-based traumatic stress."* All staff would have to make anti-racism statements.

Student courses had to focus on *"Black liberation"* and *"challenges to white supremacy,"* while overhauling the entire curriculum, reading lists, and student plays to reflect diversity and social justice themes. If the performance of black students was not equivalent with other students in any high-level academic courses by 2023, then those courses had to be abolished.

Amidst the inability of any country to find cohesion amidst racial diversity, nationalism and supremacy flourished among other races, becoming more emboldened. Wanting more from white people united them, until white people have nothing left to give.

White America continued weakening, at war with herself. As Trump left office in January 2021, the Proud Boys scorned Trump on Telegram social media. *"Trump will go down as a total failure."*

15. IDENTITY POLITICS

In 1977, the Combahee River Collective of black socialist lesbian feminists in Boston issued the Combahee River Collective Statement, introducing talk of identity politics. It invited voters and political parties to choose candidates by their identities.

Identity politics presumes that political candidates best represent voters, or only represent voters, when they share a common identity. Identity nationalism necessitates identity politics. Identity politics fuels identity nationalism.

Both result from a lack of an overarching common identity, as is inevitable amidst racial diversity. Racial diversity necessitates identity politics.

Condemning identity politics is hanging onto Western post-racial dreams of globalism uniting everyone on earth, individualism separating everyone on earth, or civic nationalism uniting citizens of a country across different races. Globalism, individualism, and civic nationalism fail, because human beings are naturally racist.

Disregarding race, President Reagan presumed their conservative values made Hispanics Republican without them yet knowing it. His amnesty to illegal immigrants might have increased Republican support among Hispanics, but most Hispanics remained Democrat. Reagan grew the Hispanic voting blocs, in time delivering his Californian home state to Democrats.

Condemning identity politics is hoping that voters, employers, and sports team selectors choose between candidates of different races according to merit. If they do, people complain.

People of other races choosing candidates of their race are called representative democracy. White people choosing white candidates would be called racism. For white people to play in the places where identity politics rules, being any place with racial diversity, they need identities other than race.

Identity politics is racism and sexism. It is discrimination by race, religion, gender, sexuality, and everything else accorded an identity.

Wealthy white women who refuse for themselves racial identities insist upon gender identities instead. Gender and sexuality become for white people what race remains for other races, although they might alienate more voters, especially from other races, than they attract.

In 2008, America elected Obama president because he was black. In 2016, she elected Trump because he was white. In 2020, she elected Biden because he was not Trump.

All three represented change from the trajectories America was taking. Obama represented change because of his race. Trump represented change because of his apparent nationalism. Biden represented change because he was not Trump.

Not that anyone admitted those reasons for electing Obama or Trump. Voters unashamedly declared that reason for electing Biden. Americans remained free to declare they wanted change, even if they did not admit the changes they wanted.

Trump's opponent in 2016 was also white, but Hillary Clinton did not exude the pride in being American or comfort in being white that Trump exuded: the nationalism and racism. Neither did any other Republican candidate but Trump.

She also talked up being a woman: her gender identity. Clinton's campaign slogans included *"I'm With Her."* Candidates do not need to mention their gender for voters to know.

Clinton's gender was not the change that she might have thought it would be. She promised more of the same, a third Obama term, but the same was not working for large numbers of Americans. In 2020, after four years of Trump, a third Obama term did not seem so bad.

Data from the Stanford University and University of Michigan collaboration American National Election Studies suggested a greater preference among women for Republicans from 1952 to 1962. That might have been because Democrats were closer to trade unions and other organized labor, focused upon men's wages and working conditions.

President Johnson ensured minority race voting rights with the Voting Rights Act of 1965, reinforcing Democrats' burgeoning preference for advancing other races instead of defending white workers. Increasingly from 1964 onwards, and especially since the 1980s when the Republican Party became opposed to abortion rights, there has been a greater preference among women for

Democrats.

Traditionally, women saw war as men protecting them by military means, but they also feared for their husbands and sons. Instead of fighting, white women increasingly wanted America to submit to other races and religions. If that submission did not bring peace, then it made conflict less violent.

White men were less submissive than white women to other races and religions. Men became more likely to vote Republican.

According to the Roper Center at Cornell University, New York, more white voters voted for the Republican nominee than the Democratic nominee at every presidential election from 1976, the first year for which it reported such data. Every Democrat elected president was elected because of his support from other races.

Immigration to a democracy with universal suffrage delivers political power to immigrant races. White Americans resenting their disenfranchisement should be no surprise. White Americans celebrating their disenfranchisement is extraordinary.

Other races also celebrate white people's disenfranchisement. *"The Old White Man's Last Hurrah,"* declared *Time* magazine of Trump in February 2016. *"Clinton now has her entire candidacy riding on voters of color,"* enthused Sally Kohn, a lesbian Jewess, *"especially older black men and women more accustomed to a lifetime of their votes being taken for granted."*

She dismissed white people, as no other race allowed itself to be dismissed. Democrats were much newer than Republicans to a disinterest in poor and working class white people, but in their rush to embrace other races, as well as professional white women and sexual minorities, Democrats progressed quickly through disinterest to thinly veiled contempt for the people they saw as America's past, but not her future.

Advisers among Hillary Clinton's inner circle reputedly felt they did not need, or even want, voters once the core of the Democratic Party. Hearing them was Clinton's husband Bill, born in out-of-the-way Arkansas in 1946, when America's rich still gave her poor a chance to succeed. Clinton's father was a travelling salesman who died before he was born. His mother was a nursing student.

His wife's greatest advocate, Clinton reputedly said, or thought, that Democrats were dismissing people like him. Hillary Clinton chose white Virginia senator Tim Kaine as her vice-presidential running mate.

That Trump was so identified with white people made hostility to white people hostility to Trump, and vice versa. All the force bearing down upon white people daring to defend their race and culture bore down upon Trump's supporters, for much the same reason. It might have done more than anything Trump ever did to talk up his nationalism.

The only thing worse for some people than admitting they wanted immigration cut, knowing the fury that engendered in the West, was admitting they supported Trump. That was no coincidence.

A car bumper sticker reputedly called upon people to vote for Trump: no one else would know. Polling booths were private, secretive spaces.

The shy Trump voter was the shy Republican voter and then some. In 2016, normally reliable exit polling failed, possibly because many people voting for Trump were suspicious of pollsters.

American-born Armenian Ana Kasparian understood the name of *The Young Turks* program, on which she became a hostess in 2008, to refer to rebels rather than Turks, although one of its creators was Turkish-born Cenk Uygur. On the night of the 2016 election, Kasparian described an incident while she was queuing to vote that day.

"...and as I was waiting in line," said Kasparian, "there were two older white guys. They're, they're behind me, and in the span of five minutes they bad-mouthed Latinos, loudly, and very transparently, bad-mouthed Latinos, Muslims, and black people, okay, and I just couldn't take it anymore, and I just turned around and I told them to shut the F up. We wouldn't have experienced that before, like that kind of open hatred where you feel emboldened enough to talk like that about three groups of people in the country that are different from you and, and it just scares me. I don't want to live in a country like that."

Those older white men were not listened to, as the grievances of every other race were listened to. They were told to shut up.

Nobody told Kasparian to shut up. That she might not want to live in America would not have troubled those older white men, but they had nowhere else to go. They did not have the choices that her parents made when they came to America.

In spite of his promises upon which Trump was elected, Trump's presidency returned to the Republican Party's failed bids to court other races. Exemplifying Trump's efforts to woo black voters, he feted black musician Kanye West in the Oval Office in October 2018 to discuss manufacturing, policing, and mental health. The two showmen clowned around.

Trump hosted a gathering of racial minorities on the South Lawn of the White House in October 2020, which two thousand people reportedly attended. *"Ignoring all press inquiries,"* tweeted black conservative commentator Candace Owens the previous day. *"Big day tomorrow... #BLEXIT @BLEXIT @realDonaldTrump."*

Blexit was the exit of black people from the Democratic Party. Trump lost in 2020 because of Wexit: white people's exit from Trump.

Political candidates seeking the support of other races are one thing. Doing so at the expense of their race is another.

Trump took white votes for granted in 2020, much as Democrats took Wisconsin, Michigan, and Pennsylvania for granted in 2016. Democrats learnt the lesson of the 2016 election that Trump did not appreciate. White people still mattered.

Among the white men who Hillary Clinton's campaign dismissed in 2016 were men like Joe Biden. Born in Scranton, Pennsylvania in 1942, his father once wealthy struggled to find regular work. If the Obama presidency invited Trump to stand and win in 2016, then the Trump presidency invited Obama's vice president Biden to stand and win in 2020.

No longer was being a woman or racial minority the key to political and other success, let alone being a Muslim, homosexual, or so-called transgendered. Trump made being a white male Christian the path for Democrats to recover the White House. Most other demographics were voting Democrat anyway, but Biden was the chance to peel back white people dissatisfied with Trump's time in office. Biden might only peel back a small portion of white people, but that would be enough.

In April 2019, Biden announced his candidacy for president. Trump continued chasing black votes.

"...the 1994 Crime Bill that Sleepy Joe Biden was so heavily involved in passing," Trump tweeted in May 2019. *"That was a dark period in American History, but has Sleepy Joe apologized? No!"*

In 1994, Republicans led the popular Violent Crime Control

and Law Enforcement Act, which Biden, President Clinton, and other Democrats supported. It tightened criminal sentencing laws.

"Anyone associated with the 1994 Crime Bill will not have a chance of being elected," Trump tweeted an hour later. *"In particular, African Americans will not be able to vote for you. I, on the other hand, was responsible for Criminal Justice Reform, which had tremendous support, & helped fix the bad 1994 Bill!"*

Trump sounded like a Democrat. Biden sounded like a Republican.

Biden was the Democrats' identity candidate for 2020. In spite of him selecting mixed-race woman Kamala Harris to be his vice-presidential nominee, the Democratic National Convention in 2020 dwelt upon white people, especially white men.

The Republican National Convention in 2020 focused upon other races, and Trump's family. "I am the least racist person in this room," Trump told Biden at Belmont University, Tennessee in October 2020, in their last presidential debate.

Oblivious to the voters who supported Trump in 2016 after he was called racist, Trump kept giving white people more reason to support Biden. Many white people recognized racism to be a word manipulating them into giving more to other races. Amidst their declining lives, white people with little left to give could do with some white racism in Washington.

In 2020, both sides got what they wanted. Using exit polls, the Brookings Institution in Washington estimated that Trump gained six percent of the black vote, five percent of the Latino or Hispanic vote, and eleven percent of the Asian vote from 2016 to 2020. Biden gained three percent of the white vote over Clinton, thereby winning the election.

Biden gained most votes among white men, Trump's largest support base. He gained eleven percent among college graduates and six percent among men without college degrees.

By nominating a white heterosexual Christian male comfortable with his biological gender to stand against another in the 2020 election, as all major party presidential nominees had been before 2008, Democrats had taken identity politics off the table. That left policy, personality, and competence.

The 2016 election had been a rare presidential election in which policy was important, but Trump's principal policies of 2016 were rarely mentioned in 2020. The only policy Trump felt he needed in

2020 was America First: nationalism. It was the Trump presidency: big on message, light on action.

Fundamental as America First was, it was not the specific policies of 2016. It was necessary but not enough in an election in which Democrats were not rejecting America First. When America was great, Democrats put America First.

In 2020, Democrats too said little about policy. Biden was not about to build a wall along the Mexican border or deport millions of illegal immigrants, but by 2020, neither was Trump.

Beyond the platitudes of bringing Americans together, Biden minimized, played down, or sidestepped major policy differences with Trump, preferring talk of task forces to specific promises. Periodically he raised some policies, most notably around environmentalism, but they were not central to the contest. He did not repudiate Trump's nationalism, although he quietly promised to review or repeal parts of it. He was a consensus man, standing for decency more than policy.

For many voters who supported Trump, 2020 was again an election about policy: the policies with which they associated Trump from four years earlier. Trump might have won the 2020 election had he fought it on policy, but he did not.

That policy was not on the table in 2020 was acknowledgement by Biden that nationalism was attractive, at least to white America. By Biden keeping away from contentious policy differences, only personality and competence remained.

Without significant policy differences between presidential candidates Al Gore and George W Bush in 2000, experts said that likeability would decide the outcome. All else being equal, which candidate did voters most want to see on their television screens, in their lounge rooms?

Both had political experience. Both enjoyed stable and loving marriages, extremely unlikely to suffer the infidelity that tainted Bill Clinton's candidacy in 1992 and would rock his presidency. After the past few years of scandal, which candidate in 2000 did voters expect to see less often?

If Gore had a fault, he was wooden, aside from his passionate kiss of wife Tipper at the 2000 Democratic National Convention. It assured voters that he would not repeat the scandals of the Clinton era.

The choice in 2000 was difficult. The result was close.

Days before the 2016 election, a Gallup poll found that fifty-two percent of adult Americans had an unfavorable view of Hillary Clinton. It was the second highest rating since Gallup started polling favorability and unfavorability in 1956. Trump's rating was sixty-one percent, but he had policy on his side.

A Gallup poll in September 2020 found that sixty-six percent of adult Americans considered Biden likeable. Only thirty-six percent considered Trump likeable.

Biden was a nicer person than Trump, with a personal story overcoming hardship that appealed to American nationalists, and others. Biden was the candidate that voters most wanted to see, if they had to see any.

For many voters who supported Biden, the 2020 election was about character. Trump played to that, oblivious to people's impression of Trump's character. Trump had long made his presidency personal.

Not simply brash, Trump was obnoxious. Facing a candidate they liked and another candidate they disliked in 2020, numerous Americans voted for the candidate they disliked, perhaps gritting their teeth as they did, but not enough for Trump to win.

The ideal candidate in 2020 might well have been Biden with Trump's policies carried forward from 2016. Such a candidate did not exist, but Biden and Trump saying so little about policy was the next best thing for Biden.

Biden might have been too polite to defeat any other president but Trump. He needed Trump's off-putting personality and incompetence to speak for themselves.

"The presidential race was more a referendum on a person," Utah senator Mitt Romney told the *Meet the Press* television program after the election, "and when it comes to policy, we did pretty well."

In 2018, Democrats angry for having lost the presidency in 2016 turned out in force for the mid-term Congressional elections. Mid-term elections are normally rough for whichever party is in the White House, and this was particularly brutal. In a system that rewards incumbency, Republicans lost their majority in the House of Representatives they had held since the mid-term elections in President Obama's first term, eight years earlier.

The Senate was easier for Republicans in 2018, because the Democrats had done so well twelve years earlier, in the mid-term elections of President George W Bush's second term. With fewer Republican Senate seats to defend in 2018, Democrats did well, without gaining Senate control.

In 2020, Republicans had more senators to defend. Pundits predicted a blue wave delivering the Senate to Democrats, while forecasting increased Democrat control in the House. As votes transpired, Republicans took fourteen House seats from Democrats, losing three. Republicans lost two Senate seats in November 2020, each of which had peculiar circumstances, and recovered a lost seat in Alabama.

Trump the person was the problem, not his policies. Congressional Republicans campaigned on general Republican Party principles and the same America First platform as Trump, adopted at the Republican National Convention that year. The platform was sound because nationalism is sound. The problem with Trump-ism was Trump.

16. RE-ELECTION

In March 2018, Trump nominated John Bolton as National Security Advisor. In September 2019, Trump tweeted that he dismissed Bolton. Bolton would say that he resigned.

"There really isn't any guiding principle that I was able to discern other than what's good for Donald Trump's re-election," Bolton said of Trump to Martha Raddatz of *ABC News* in June 2020. "…there's no coherent basis, no strategy, no philosophy."

An American nationalist ought to convey a sense that America's and Americans' interests are guiding principles: America First. Trump did not convey that sense to his National Security Advisor.

"A lot of people have complained that he has a short attention span and he doesn't focus," said Bolton. "When it comes to re-election, his attention span is infinite."

For a man so proudly not a politician, Trump acted like a politician. To the extent that politics is promising, campaigning, and narrative, Trump over performed, if only in the time he expended at them.

Trump never ceased being a candidate. He never became president.

The best campaign for re-election an elected official can make is to perform well in office. Elected officials determine their re-electability. No media campaigns or political plots deny an elected official re-election who has earned re-election. Elections are for incumbents to win or lose.

Challengers depend first upon an incumbent's performance. It is very difficult for challengers to dislodge successful incumbents.

External factors do not cost elected officials re-election. Their responses to those factors might.

Challengers react to incumbents. They can identify incumbents' failings and bring them to voters' attention. They can recognize incumbents' strengths, but find niches by which those challengers position themselves as better, even if only slightly better, alternatives in voters' minds.

Voters love being happy whatever the outcome of an election. They dread being unhappy whatever the outcome.

Successful officials and administrations stand on their record, but voters do not simply reward them by re-electing them. Voters conclude from their success that they will continue to succeed. People vote for the future, not the past.

Every election can be won. Every election can be lost.

From an incumbent's viewpoint, there is no weaker place to stand than relying upon frightening the electorate about a challenger. Scare campaigns can work, but good officials and administrations do not need them. It is the weakest of re-election tactics, reserved to the weakest of elected officials. Any incumbent relying upon frightening the electorate about electing a challenger does not deserve re-election.

In October 2020, a Gallup poll reported that fifty-six percent of American voters believed Trump did not deserve re-election. A substantial number of Americans voted to re-elect him without believing he deserved re-election.

In the absence of a scare campaign or something similar taking hold, voters still undecided close to Election Day tend to break towards challengers. Incumbents failing to persuade voters to re-elect them, voters tend to give challengers a chance. Those challengers had also failed to persuade them, but voters recognize the benefits of incumbency. They impose a higher standard of persuasion upon incumbents than challengers.

President Obama might have delivered less than his most optimistic supporters wanted of him, but he had never promised what they wanted: to save the world. He probably would not have become president if he had.

In the 2016 election, there was technically no incumbent, but Hillary Clinton ran an incumbent's campaign. One president did not make the Clintons a political dynasty, although Hillary's prominence in her husband's presidency, eight years in the Senate, and four years as Secretary of State brought them close. Two presidents would be a dynasty. The former First Lady offered a return to the Clinton presidency, or four more years of the Obama presidency.

She was the establishment's Democratic candidate, offering continuity with past presidencies. When Trump became the presumptive Republican nominee, she became the establishment candidate.

In 2016, minor-party and undecided voters numbered fifteen percent of likely voters two weeks from Election Day, according to statistician Nate Silver. A post-election survey by the Pew Research Center in Washington found that they broke heavily towards Trump, even more so than voters normally broke to challengers. Voters with low or no expectations of either candidate gave the outsider Trump a chance. They were not devoted to him, and might not have particularly liked him, but they did not hate him.

Politics, like business, is often a matter of managing expectations. During the 2016 campaign, Trump set his supporters high expectations for his presidency: that he would make America great again.

Having won, Trump could have deflated voters' expectations, talking of the challenges before him and before America. That could have let him by 2020 seem successful for having met, or even exceeded, those lower expectations.

He never did. Trump failed to achieve his lofty commitments in 2016 and throughout his presidency.

A re-election campaign based upon high expectations was always going to struggle among voters whose expectations were not met. Expectations of a second Trump term were lower than they needed to be, except to Trump.

In 2020, minor-party and undecided voters were much fewer than they had been in 2016. In a referendum about the outsider-president Trump, the Washington-insider Biden was not obviously a challenger.

Trump's rallies of 2016 had been entertaining cases for his election with commentary about America's and Americans' plight, with promises to redress to them. There was more reason and intellect than Trump's critics acknowledged.

His words felt spontaneous and sincere, personal chats with everyone there and with people watching through their television sets and computer screens. Audiences felt part of a movement, as nationalism was in 2016.

The rallies continued while Trump was in office, saying much of Trump's preference for campaigning over governing. Although they were much less frequent than they had been before his election, they remained extraordinarily frequent.

They were times for Trump to revel in the enthusiasm of his

supporters, but they could not teach him anything, except that his promises remained popular. "Build the wall," people chanted, giving Trump the euphoria of building a wall along the Mexican border without actually building it.

The approval of the crowd, the adoring mob, mattered to him, but they were strangers to him. The rallies were not opportunities for voters to tell Trump anything he did not already know. He provided the cues, to which the throngs yelled their approval or disapproval.

They gave Trump no information. The very nature of a rally meant that people joined a multitude. With little new for Trump to say, they became solely emotive experiences, not intellectual, much like crowds at football games yelling love and hate they do not mean, and a short time later cannot recall.

They were chances for Trump to assure people that he thought every day of them, not of the people in Washington. It was an affirmation of nationalism, but nationalism and everything else of substance is not simply making an impression. It is doing something. The time that Trump spent addressing rallies was time he did not spend delivering on that nationalism: doing in Washington what he had promised to do and claimed to be doing.

By October 2020, the rallies were streams of consciousness of Trump's thoughts and feelings. The less a person has to say, the longer he takes to say it.

"I feel so powerful," he told a rally outside Orlando, eleven days after announcing he had been infected with the Wuhan virus.

If a candidate is an issue in an election, then candidates normally want another candidate to be the issue. So much the narcissist, Trump kept himself the issue.

"Could you imagine if I lose?" Trump asked a rally in Macon, Georgia, in October 2020. "My whole life – what am I going to do? I'm going to say I lost to the worst candidate in the history of politics. I am not going to feel so good, maybe I will have to leave the country, I don't know."

Gone was the cry of "I love the poorly educated," from four years earlier. Gone too was the commentary about America and Americans.

Still Trump talked of the wall he said he was building. "Build the wall," the masses still chanted, urging him and Congress along.

There were no new promises in 2020 like those that Trump

made in 2016. Having failed to implement past promises, there was not any point. Making more promises might remind people of his promises not kept.

What remained was still the euphoria, the belonging of being part of a movement, but only for the people who attended the rallies. For television and computer viewers, it was all less entertaining.

The rallies might have pumped up people to get out and vote, but delivering promises in the preceding four years would have done that. There was no reason for anyone new to join.

Because voters vote for the future, the election campaign that matters is the current one. Trump's 2020 campaign was the very opposite of his 2016 campaign, which might have been the reason he retreated to fighting his 2016 rival, reliving the glory of a campaign he won, but not the campaign he was supposed to be waging.

In 2016, Trump had reason to make whatever political capital he could from Hillary Clinton's electronic mail during her tenure as Secretary of State, which ended in 2013. It might have helped neutralize character as an issue, if Trump and Clinton were no better than the other, but if it played to matters of character, then that was not where Trump won the election.

Clinton campaigning for Biden in 2020 did not make her the candidate, but Trump was still worrying about her mail. Trump was still inviting his rallies to call for Clinton to be locked up, although he had been in office for almost four years without Clinton being charged with a crime. Trump's rallies were like raucous crowds watching boxing contests, but with only one boxer in the ring.

In 2020, Trump's obsession with Clinton's mail was bizarre. He had no votes to gain, no money to make, by his unending campaign against her. If he thought that it fired up his core supporters to vote, then he thought they had little else to fire them.

Trump's attacks on Hillary Clinton were a vendetta against an American against whom Trump had no reason to have a vendetta. She had not wronged him. She had simply stood in an election against him that he won. If anything, he should have appreciated her more than he did, for having lost.

It presented Trump as a man in his own space, instead of the national space. It reminded voters that Trump's interests were not primarily the nation. His primary interest was Trump.

From early 2018, Trump's campaign slogan for 2020 had been to *"Keep America Great,"* as it would for a president insisting that he had made America great again. The usual pitch for re-election by a president in a country in which by custom and then by law a president served no more than two terms was always some expression of more of the same.

The crises of 2020 ended that. Linking to an *Associated Press* report titled 'Virus, racial unrest force Trump campaign to recalibrate' in June 2020, the *Drudge Report* included the small heading *"KEEP AMERICA GREAT,"* but with a line through it: *"KEEP AMERICA GREAT."* The 2020 election was one for striking words and letters through.

Trump toyed with *"Make America Great Again, Again."* It would have claimed the first three years of his presidency made America great again while acknowledging the calamity of the Wuhan virus, but he never acknowledged that calamity.

Whether on economic grounds, political grounds, or more likely both, Trump wanted optimism. Optimism accelerates economies and wins elections, but Trump never found the words to convey that optimism. He never found another message.

What remained was *"Make America Great Again."* It was all too much like 2016, with nothing new to say.

The man who campaigned so well in 2016 campaigned poorly in 2020. In July 2020, Trump's campaign released an advertisement showing images of riots in America in May 2020. "You won't be safe in Joe Biden's America," the advertisement warned, oblivious to Trump being president.

Almost four years had passed since Biden ceased being vice president. In 2020, he held no elected office.

When confronted with questions about his use of social media and name-calling in an interview on the *60 Minutes* television program late in October 2020, Trump did not take the chance to explain his behavior to voters in the television audience. Instead, he walked away. He walked away from every voter thinking the same questions.

Fundamentally, election campaigns ought to convince people to vote for a person or political party. In countries with voluntary voting, they ought to convince people to vote.

Trump might have felt he had no need to make a case for his re-election. So convinced was he of his success and Biden's failings, he seems to have felt assured of re-election. Thus he could continue doing as he had always done: doing whatever he wanted to do. He campaigned as he liked to campaign, without thought of persuading the voters. Hubris brings down more political careers than does incompetence.

Tens of millions of Americans had decided to vote for Trump before the 2020 campaign began. Trump's campaign gave undecided voters no more reasons to vote for him. It gave voters who had settled upon Biden no reason to change their mind. People voting for Trump found reasons to do so that he did not articulate.

Campaigning against Trump in 2020, critics condemned him for his broken promises from 2016: not building the wall, not draining the swamp, not ending the endless wars, and so forth. There was great irony in people condemning Trump for not honoring promises they deeply opposed anyway, but their purpose was to ween Trump's supporters from him. Biden might have been more likely to deliver at least something of what Trump promised in 2016 than Trump would be in a second term, having failed to deliver it in his first.

Trump's loss in 2020 was not a defeat of his policies from 2016. It was a defeat of his failure to honor those policies.

Were anyone but Trump the president in 2020, he would have been vulnerable to the criticisms at which Trump excelled. Conversely, a hypothetical citizen Trump would have been the ideal challenger to bring down an incumbent president like Trump had been, far more scathing of the Trump presidency than Biden was, or indeed any other political candidate would have been.

For the most part, the people who hated Trump for the promises he made in 2016 hated him for making them. They did not cease hating him because he failed to honor them.

He had not renounced his policies, so they had no reason to forgive him. The people hating American nationalism and America were unforgiving anyway.

Making those promises won Trump the election in 2016. Not renouncing them, but leaving them in the air for people to think he might honor them in a second term let Trump retain most of his support in 2020.

Had Trump kept his major promises he made before the 2016 election, then he would have exuded the same nationalism in 2020 that he exuded in 2016. His presidency would have been a success, probably securing his re-election.

The ten-percent nationalism that Trump exuded in 2020 was enough to earn the second largest vote in American history, but it was not enough to win. His failure to honor his promises only cost him a small percentage of his support, but it cost him enough to cost him the election. Voters had memories of his rhetoric, but knowledge of how little of it he acted upon.

It takes a lot for an American president to fail to be re-elected. Trump achieved it, against a weaker challenger than President Carter faced in 1980 or President George H W Bush faced in 1992.

The remarkable aspect of the 2020 result was not that Trump lost, but that he polled as well as he did. Enough hope remained in the promises he made in 2016, and those promises remained good enough, for almost half of American voters to wish him a second term. The promise of nationalism was better than none.

Never before might an American president have commanded so much constant attention with so many words and so little work. For all the drama of Trump's term in office, nothing much was done.

By 2000, eight years of drama and scandal had left Americans with a certain Clinton fatigue, in spite of the high approval President Clinton enjoyed. Trump produced more fatigue in four years.

When the 2020 election rolled around, many voters felt weary of the chaos and conflict on which Trump thrived. Trump's critics might not have felt it, but their hatred of him, from which they never tired, drove them.

Biden offered a return to presidencies before Trump, when presidents were normally seen and heard only when they had something useful to say. For many of Trump's supporters, the bitter disappointment of his loss in 2020 turned to relief that the drama was over. If there was to be no real change, then the inconsequential spectacle had been pointlessly exhausting. The noise for so little return had passed.

There was also the gutting pain of knowing that a chance, perhaps the last chance, to save America had been wasted. Trump never really paid attention, before Biden returned America to her orderly decline.

17. DEMOCRACY

Democracy depends on nationalism. Candidates and voters must act lawfully and respect election results.

Lyndon Johnson appeared to have lost the 1948 election for a Senate seat from Texas. Six days after polls closed, more than two hundred additional ballots were found in Precinct 13, Jim Wells County, all of which favored Johnson. Johnson won.

In the 1960 presidential election, Johnson was John Kennedy's vice-presidential running mate. In spite of evidence of fraud in the vote-counting giving Kennedy victory, especially in Texas and Illinois, Republican nominee Richard Nixon conceded defeat. Nixon told journalist Earl Mazo that "our country cannot afford the agony of a constitutional crisis." Sometime later, Nixon lost his way.

Losing nationalism, America descended into factions. Rival political camps fought back and forth, becoming increasingly polarized.

House of Representatives Republicans impeached President Clinton in 1998. House Democrats impeached Trump in 2019.

Ordinary voters opposed both impeachments. The impassioned bases of each impeaching party loved them.

That Trump won the Electoral College but lost the popular vote in 2016 was as immaterial as it was to George W Bush's victory in 2000. America's voting system is the Electoral College, much as Britain's voting system is parliamentary. Political parties and candidates campaign accordingly.

Die-hard Democrats spent the first term of George W Bush's presidency denying that Bush was president. The Supreme Court refused Al Gore the counting of votes he wanted.

Die-hard Republicans spent Obama's presidency denying that Obama was president because he was foreign born, pursuant to Article II of the Constitution. Obama was not foreign born, but with an American mother, he was eligible to be president even if he was foreign born.

Amidst the hostility to Trump and his supporters, pundits warned of violence after his inevitable election loss in 2016. After Trump won, his opponents ran amok.

Ordinary voters had no bar with any of it. Ordinary voters rarely entered into it.

Having arrogantly dismissed opinion polling that he would lose the looming 2020 election, Trump had every reason to be certain of victory. The fears expressed before the 2016 election of Trump's brut aggression had long looked unfounded.

In the weeks before the 2020 election, Trump signs disappeared from outside people's homes. His critics concluded that voters were turning away from him, but they might simply have feared another bout from Trump's opponents on election night if Trump won, much like the angry violence through much of 2020 from Black Lives Matter and Antifa.

After Trump lost, there was no violence. Tens of millions of Americans were bitterly disappointed with the result, devastated even, but nationalists do not recklessly damage the country in which they believe. Patriots do not destroy the country they love.

They might protest, waving placards. They might tweet or post messages on social media, as much for people agreeing with them as for people disagreeing with them. They might brandish their guns, not to use but to demonstrate to the new administration that it will not take those guns from them.

There were not the tears of pain like those broadcast on social media following Trump's victory four years earlier. Patriotic disappointment is felt more privately.

Trump's opponents demonstrated their lack of nationalism by refusing to respect the 2016 election results. Unable to believe Trump had won, they spent four years claiming that Russian influence invalidated Trump's win.

Trump demonstrated his lack of nationalism by refusing to respect the 2020 election results. Unable to believe he had lost, Trump claimed that widespread electoral fraud invalidated Biden's win.

In December 2016, Martin Sheen and other actors and actresses issued a short video titled *A Message for Electors to Unite for America*. They called upon the Electoral College not to elect Trump the president.

After the 2020 election, Trump called upon state governors and legislatures to appoint presidential electors supporting him. After the Electoral College elected Biden president in December 2020, Trump called upon Congress and Vice President Pence not to confirm that election when they met in January 2021 to count the Electoral College votes and declare the election winner.

America was in a revolving cycle. Countries in decline often are.

For much of 2020, Trump had focused not on for whom people voted, or even whether they voted. Instead, he focused upon the mechanism by which they voted.

Postal voting, or mail-in voting, had become increasingly more common in America for many years. The pandemic added to its use in 2020.

Mail-in voting increased voting by people otherwise less likely to vote. Those people were more likely to vote Democrat. There was thus good reason for Democrats to widen postal voting and for Republicans to narrow it, although Utah legislators felt secure enough to offer it to all counties there.

Biden called upon people supporting him to vote promptly, in person or by mail. He thus secured their votes. They could not change their votes if they changed their minds.

In August 2020, Trump voted by mail in Florida. Nevertheless, in spite of mail-in voting assisting people in remote locations and the elderly and infirmed to vote, Trump continued campaigning against mail-in voting. Explicitly and implicitly, he discouraged his supporters from mail-in voting.

They could vote in person early or on Election Day, but voting in person was the imposition that mail-in voting redressed. Deferring their vote allowed people time to change their minds, or to become too busy or unwell to vote. If people who would have voted for Trump by mail ultimately voted for Biden or did not vote at all, then Trump might have cost himself re-election.

Trump's campaign was against mail-in voting. It should have been against Biden.

Votes cast in person in 2020 were extraordinarily skewed towards Trump, which allowed him to claim on election night that he had won. The millions of mail-in votes counted through the days thereafter were extraordinarily skewed towards Biden.

Voters and losing candidates want allegations of fraud or error investigated. They seek evidence, but there was no evidence of widespread fraud or error behind Trump's loss. Allegations do not make something true.

Votes apparently cast by dead people might have incorrectly recorded votes by surviving family members. The numbers were tiny.

Allegations of postal workers diverting ballot papers or being instructed to place false date stamps on envelopes were recanted upon inquiry by official investigators. Video alleged to show electoral fraud did not.

There has probably been voter fraud in every election through the decades leading up to 2020, amounting to hundreds of votes across America. Trump lost by tens of thousands of votes in even the closest contested states.

Trump also challenged in-person voting. In Antrim County, Michigan, a discrepancy in vote tallies revealed a clerical error, corrected within hours.

Many states and counties used machines and computer software from Dominion Voting Systems of Ontario, Canada and Colorado. *"REPORT: DOMINION DELETED 2.7 MILLION TRUMP VOTES NATIONWIDE,"* tweeted Trump in November 2020. *"DATA ANALYSIS FINDS 221,000 PENNSYLVANIA VOTES SWITCHED FROM PRESIDENT TRUMP TO BIDEN. 941,000 TRUMP VOTES DELETED. STATES USING DOMINION VOTING SYSTEMS SWITCHED 435,000 VOTES FROM TRUMP TO BIDEN."*

Did Trump believe that Dominion thought removing him from office was worth destroying its billion-dollar business? Dominion depended upon its reputation for integrity.

The Federal Bureau of Investigation and Department of Justice investigated Trump's claims. They dismissed them.

"This is total fraud," Trump told *Fox News* late in November 2020, "and how the F.B.I. and Department of Justice, I don't know, maybe they're involved...."

The claim would have been astonishing from an unsuccessful challenger, but Trump was the president, administering those agencies. If voting processes were vulnerable to fraud, Trump had had four years in office to deal with them.

Trump's claims of massive, probably orchestrated, fraud against him cemented his outsider status: that he had so threatened powerful people they removed him. Instead of being a loser he abhorred, he was a victim: a winner and a victim.

Whether Trump believed his allegations, only he knew, but good people trusted him, salvaging something of his reputation. Others became uncertain, seeing him a little less of a loser than they might otherwise have seen him.

After the 2000 election, Al Gore took court action seeking to overturn the count in a single state, Florida, decided by a small margin of votes. Determining what votes were valid and the right of the Secretary of State in Florida to conclude counting and declare the winner were specific issues under Florida law. Gore lost.

Overturning the results in one state would not deliver Trump the presidency in 2020. He challenged the results in several battleground states. Amidst his many legal actions, Trump's only success was minor. Trump lost.

The possibility of fraud is not proof of fraud. A lack of confidence in the integrity of a voting system is not tantamount to fraud.

Republicans around America tried to tread a path connecting Trump's claims with reason. Voters and losing candidates want laws and procedures providing them with confidence in the integrity of voting. The lack of evidence of widespread fraud did not amount to proof there was no widespread fraud.

The result of the 2000 election rode upon chads and hanging chads in voting cards in Florida, waking states and counties across America to modernize their voting methods. Voting processes might need constant review for improvement, but Trump was not looking to improve the conduct of future elections. He wanted to overturn the preceding election.

Media reports gave little indication of any other interest from the White House, while the pandemic took more American lives each week than it had previously taken. President-elect Biden announced measures related to the pandemic and pending appointees.

Congress passed bills providing pandemic relief paying six hundred dollars to every American. Trump, staying at his Mar-a-Lago estate in Florida, called for that to be increased to two thousand dollars.

Trump's call might have been nationalism. It would aid America's poor.

It might have been individualism. Americans would like him for it.

It might also have been malice, adding to Biden's burden in the presidency. America's national debt was approaching twenty-eight trillion dollars, after being less than twenty trillion dollars when Trump took office.

Trump might simply have been keeping attention upon himself. Normally, a president-elect enjoys national attention, but Biden could not displace Trump from the spotlight.

That might have been a service to Biden. He planned and carried out his transition more thoughtfully than Trump carried out his transition four years earlier.

Ahead in January 2021 were run-off elections for the two Georgia Senate seats. After the first round of voting in November, the Republican candidates were favored to win.

Retaining the Senate in the face of a Democratic president could have inspired Republicans to vote in the run-off elections, as could avenging any sense they had been cheated in November. Continued feelings among Democrats that Gore had been cheated of the presidency in 2000 motivated Democrats to vote in the 2002 mid-term Congressional elections, although the 2001 Muslim terror attacks on America overshadowed them.

Trump's continuing efforts to overturn his loss diminished those motivations. At what was called a press conference but was more of a small rally in Atlanta in December 2020, lawyer Lin Wood called upon the two Republican candidates in Georgia to call upon the Georgia legislature to appoint electors for Trump. "If they do not do it," Wood told Georgia voters, "they have not earned your vote. Don't you give it to them."

Telling Republicans that Georgia elections were unfair might also have discouraged them from voting. "Why would you go back and vote in another rigged election?" asked Wood.

Fellow lawyer Sidney Powell added: "I would encourage all Georgians to make it known that you will not vote until your vote is secure."

The two lawyers' words were not those of conservatives they said they were. Nor were they nationalist.

Trump continued assailing any Republican not submitting to his claims of fraud stealing the presidency from him. The weekend before the run-off elections, he telephoned Georgia Secretary of State Brad Raffensperger and harangued Raffensperger for more than hour to "find" Trump more votes.

With talk of Congressional Republicans not ratifying the presidential election result, and even talk of a coup keeping Trump in power, Democrats had more reason than ever to vote in Georgia. Republicans had reason to wonder whether to vote.

The Republican candidates lost both run-off elections. "This should not be close," former Republican National Committee chairman Michael Steele told the MSNBC television channel, watching the results come in. "We should be going for beers right about now because the evening would have been over, and the reality of it is, it's not, because of what this president has done to the Republican Party."

Delivering control of the Senate to Democrats aided them undoing the little Trump had done. Soon trending on Twitter was the hashtag #MAGAIsCancelled. MAGA was the longstanding acronym for Trump's catch cry "Make America Great Again." Trump seemed unconcerned.

The following day, Congress would certify Biden's win. "*Statistically impossible to have lost the 2020 Election*," Trump had tweeted late in December 2020. "*Big protest in DC on January 6th. Be there, will be wild!*"

Protestors marched upon statehouses around the country without incident. Since peaceful November, Trump had convinced them that fraud denied them democracy.

At a rally outside the White House, Trump addressed the crowd for more than an hour. "Our country has had enough," he riled up his most fervent supporters, who had travelled far to be there. "We will not take it anymore and that's what this is all about…

"We're supposed to…support our constitution, and protect our constitution…

"We're gathered together in the heart of our nation's capital for one very, very basic and simple reason, to save our democracy…

"We fight like hell and if you don't fight like hell, you're not going to have a country anymore…

"So … we're going to walk down Pennsylvania Avenue … we're going to try and give our Republicans, the weak ones, because the strong ones don't need any of our help, we're going to try and give them the kind of pride and boldness that they need to take back our country…"

Trump did not walk with them. He did not fight.

Protestors became rioters when, fired up by Trump, they stormed the Capitol Building. A plainclothes police officer shot dead an unarmed white woman, Ashli Babbitt, attempting to climb through a broken window into the House of Representatives chamber. She was aged thirty-five, married, and an Air Force veteran.

Ben Philips suffered a stroke and died. He was fifty years old, divorced, with children.

Kevin Greeson suffered a heart attack and died. He was fifty-five years old, married, with children.

Rosanne Boyland was trampled to death. Aged thirty-four, she had recovered from drug problems and become a conservative.

There was no coup. Any coup had to come from Trump, but he was secure in the West Wing of the White House, watching events on television.

There was no revolution. Revolutions normally require leadership, organization, and planning. They require work. Most Americans who voted for Trump did not think his presidency was worth joining a protest, let alone a revolution.

The day after responding to the riot, Capitol Police officer Brian Sicknick died, possibly due to a stroke. He was aged forty-two, a veteran of the Air National Guard, and also supported Trump.

Three days after responding, Capitol Police officer Howard Liebengood committed suicide. He was aged fifty-one and married. His late father served as the Senate sergeant-at-arms from 1981 until 1983 and was chief of staff to two Republican senators.

So much the individualist, so little the nationalist, Trump had given up American lives and Republican control of the Senate for any whiff of a sliver of a chance that he could overturn the 2020 election result. There had never been a whiff.

A patriot would have felt the pain of those deaths. A nationalist would not have brought those deaths about.

Nationalist leadership feels responsible for the led. Trump did not. *"The President's conduct yesterday was a betrayal of his office and supporters,"* said former attorney general William Barr in a statement.

Twitter locked Trump's personal account, before permanently suspending it. Facebook and Instagram barred Trump from posting until after Biden's inauguration.

The rioting at the Capitol Building was much less widespread, destructive, and deadly than the months of Black Lives Matter riots in 2020. People trying to understand the latter should do the same of the former.

Millions of Americans believed Trump's claims of electoral fraud because America's political, business, and religious leaders had been cheating them for years. Electoral fraud cheating Trump cheated them too. It cheated America.

American nationalists might argue against laws they feel are contrary to the national good, but they do not wantonly disobey those laws. They do not vandalize America's heritage. To have stormed the Capitol Building, decent people felt they had no other options.

"She may have laid down her rifle," Ashli Babbitt's heartbroken friend Jack Feeley told *The Sun* newspaper, "but she was still willing to lay down her life for her country and what she strongly believed in."

As the House of Representatives impeached Trump a second time, Trump set about saving himself at the expense of his supporters. "Those who engaged in the attacks last week will be brought to justice," he said in a video message.

Trump did not plead for clemency for people who trusted him. He did not pardon them.

What did Trump think would happen that day in Washington, after his complaints, court actions, and calls upon elected officials to overturn the 2020 election results? Like so much else about his presidency, his actions were not thought through. Had Trump worked as hard being president as he worked trying to overturn the 2020 results afterwards, then he might not have needed to overturn the results.

18. THE FUTURE

In 1978, Bill Clinton was elected governor of Arkansas. In 1980, he failed to be re-elected, becoming the youngest former governor in American history.

Following his defeat, Clinton did not deny his loss. He did not hide from it. He held it up inviting people to explain it to him. Travelling around Arkansas for six months late in 1981, he listened to Arkansans telling him the reasons he lost, learning from the experience.

In 1982, Clinton was again elected governor: a better candidate and governor than he had been. He remained in office for ten years until elected president in 1992. In 1996, America re-elected him.

For all their claims of Russia determining the 2016 presidential election, enough Democrats and Never-Trump Republicans accepted the reality of the result. They thus learnt from it. The outcome was the candidate and campaigning they took into the 2020 election.

Their only interest was in defeating Trump. They did.

Only from the facts can a person learn. Self-delusion denies a person the chance to learn.

To learn from a loss, a person must acknowledge that loss. Trump polled a massive number of votes in the 2020 election, in which more Americans voted than in any other election, but he lost.

Trump was not a victim of electoral fraud or anything else. The people who died because he blamed electoral fraud were victims.

For the individualist, pride and satisfaction are strictly personal. Ego takes personal success and failure to unwarranted emotional highs and lows. Americans did not used to be so egotistical, when America was great.

For the nationalist, success and failure can also be national. National pride and embarrassment moderate individual feelings.

For Trump to mock losers as cruelly and mercilessly as he did, was to set himself up for a fall. Everybody loses sometime, about something.

Trump might have seen no greater fault or weakness than losing, but there is no fault or weakness in losing. The fault or weakness is never trying. Trump tried. In 2020, he lost.

In 2016, he won. In a country in which many men and women worked long and hard to become president and never did, Trump was elected with much less work. Not being re-elected demonstrated a need for him to learn.

There is fault in losing without learning from the loss. Learning from a loss requires recognizing personal responsibility for that loss. Blaming others or blaming circumstance denies a person a chance to understand his or her failings.

All that is required of the listener is not to believe or reject everything that he or she hears. The listener needs only to consider it, perhaps remember it, to use or not use, perhaps someday to accept in whole or part or reject in whole or part. To learn requires considering criticisms on their merits, instead of suing or threatening to sue critics for libel or slander.

Learning means listening to people held in contempt, even hated. Any person on earth might teach other people something. What matters is the idea or information imparted, not the person saying it.

Presidents in office normally top surveys of the best and worst presidents in history. In the years afterwards, their polling normally moderates to the mediocrity they were, although no previous president finished his term as Trump finished his.

The much worse Black Lives Matter rioting of 2020 led to protestors' demands being met on bended knee, but that is the reality of the time. In an atmosphere in which the West has become frightened of herself, American nationalism must be peaceful, rational, and moral, if it is to be revived. Nationalism in the West ought to be peaceful, rational, and moral anyway.

Other races' nationalism does not need to be. It is unfair, but reality often is.

By the end of his term, Trump had delivered the White House and both houses of Congress to Democrats. By the worst of his behavior, he had blemished every policy he ever advocated.

Trump was not the worst president in history. He did too little for that.

It is all subjective. A person could see Abraham Lincoln as the worst president in history, for the more than six hundred thousand deaths in the unnecessary Civil War.

"While this represents the end of the greatest first term in presidential history," said Trump in a statement in the last weeks of his presidency, *"it's only the beginning of our fight to Make America Great Again!"*

Most presidential administrations were probably great by their standards and values. If the purpose of Trump's presidency was to make Trump the most famous man in the world, then it was the greatest first term in presidential history.

Trump was still making a sale. He was still in his small world.

Calling Trump's term the greatest first term in presidential history was much less incongruous than saying diversity was America's greatest strength, as Trump's critics claimed. No claim of greatness matters as do the facts, and the principles upon which claimants rely.

Through the Trump presidency, there were no great disasters, no great achievements. America was deeply divided by race, religion, region, and class before Trump's election and remained so throughout his term in office.

The circumstances in which Trump was elected in 2016 remained after his presidency finished. Trump did not make America a parlous place. He revealed what a parlous place America already was.

Trump did not help. That a man as flawed as Trump retained such devoted support among good and decent people demonstrated the depths of division in a country wrecked not by his supporters but by their leaders, Republican and Democrat alike, over decades. When champions are hard to find, desperate people take the only champion available.

That should concern America's leaders. If they want to reunite America, they need to treat a Tennessee small-town laborer with a Confederate flag on his pick-up truck as a compatriot, instead of a Guatemalan caught illegally in Santa Fe. Farmers need to employ Americans to harvest apples, even if Americans cost more than immigrants to employ. If they want America's poor and middle classes to care for them again, they need to care for America's poor and middle classes again.

Trump's loss in 2020 need not end efforts to revive American nationalism, although it could easily feel like it. Nationalism is too important, too obviously of value, to depend on any man or woman.

Late in the twentieth century, nationalism revived in Eastern Europe through the actions of many people over long periods. There were starts and setbacks, but nationalists persevered. Reviving nationalism in America will take the same.

For Trump to have a future role reviving American nationalism, he must become an American nationalist. He must take responsibility for the riot at the Capitol Building in January 2021, from which nothing good came.

Making America great again does not encompass pointless vandalism, looting, injury, or martyrdom. Empowering the powerless requires a person not to become powerless too.

Less there be any doubt that Trump was much like others of his era, his lawyers at his second trial before the Senate presented a film montage of Democrat politicians and celebrities exhorting violence against Trump and his supporters more explicitly than Trump incited insurrection before the storming of the Capitol Building. It did not diminish Trump's reckless self-indulgent stupidity after he lost the 2020 election. The difference with Trump was that otherwise peaceful people followed him.

Much worse than the violence at the Capitol Building was President George W Bush's invasion of Iraq in 2003. "The president feels each and every one of the deaths very strongly, and he grieves for their families," said White House spokeswoman Dana Perino in March 2008, when the number of Americans who Bush had sent to their deaths reached four thousand. "He obviously is grieved by the moment, but he mourns the loss of every single life."

Trump too will need to grieve for those who died at his direction. He will need to find deep regret not for his loss, but for fellow Americans' losses. Complaining that other presidents were not impeached for actions for which they might have been impeached does not detract from Trump's responsibility for being impeached, twice.

Four days after the Capitol Building riot, Trump issued a proclamation lowering American flags to half-staff, "*As a sign of respect for the service and sacrifice of United States Capitol Police Officers Brian D. Sicknick and Howard Liebengood, and all Capitol Police Officers and law enforcement across this great Nation...*" Trump offered no condolences.

Vice President Pence offered his condolences. He telephoned Sicknick's family.

"*Most recently*," said Trump's wife Melania, in a statement the day after Trump's proclamation, "*my heart goes out to: Air Force Veteran, Ashli Babbit, Benjamin Philips, Kevin Greeson, Rosanne Boyland, and Capitol Police Officers, Brian Sicknick and Howard Liebengood. I pray for their families comfort and strength during this difficult time. I am disappointed and disheartened with what happened last week.*"

Jeffrey Smith, a District of Columbia Police officer, also took his life after attending the Capitol Building riot. Metropolitan Police revealed his death later.

Relentless humility is a flaw, but humility is not a flaw. When circumstances warrant humility, humility is a virtue.

Can Trump change his personality? Everybody can. That does not mean he will.

It is not altogether clear that if Trump could relive his presidency, with all its self-aggrandizement and petty personal vendettas, then he would do anything differently. He might have liked the cameras, controversies, and attention too much to give them up to spend time accomplishing anything worthwhile. He might think that losing re-election was a price worth paying to exact revenge upon the living Jeff Sessions and dead John McCain.

Any contrition from Trump would require him to apologize in person to Sessions. It would require him to kneel at McCain's grave.

In January 2021, Canadian professor of politics Eric Kaufmann reported his results of surveying people who voted for Trump. Only twenty-nine percent wanted Trump to stand again for office. Fifty-five percent preferred "*A candidate who is more presidential, respectful and gets things done, while adopting Trump's views on controlling immigration, nationalism and being willing to challenge the mainstream media, political correctness and elites.*"

Trump's role in reviving American nationalism might not be as president again. If his contrition is sincere, he might not want it to be.

Away from politicking, Trump could return to the rational observations he made before his election but too rarely through his presidency. He could pontificate, and apply the intellect he always could apply when he wanted to apply it.

To serve and save his country, Trump's role might be campaigning for other candidates: a rally head. Trump basked in campaigning. It was governing he found tiresome.

Might America have fared better by 2021 had Ted Cruz or Chris Christie won the Republican nomination and presidency in 2016, then to have Trump from his Twitter account constantly critiquing him? Might America have fared better if Bernie Sanders won the Democrat nomination and presidency, with continuing criticism from Trump?

The most influential people through history never held elected office, but influenced people who did. Trump held it for four years. He does not need to hold office again to effect change. He can still advance the cause of American nationalism and thus America. Alternatively, he can harm them.

Has Trump made a return to nationalist government in Washington more likely, for having raised nationalist issues? Has he made it less likely, for not having been sufficient a nationalist in office?

The most pessimistic view of Trump's presidency is that it accelerated America's decline, for tarnishing American nationalism among people not knowing any better. Every venting of white America's frustrations compounded hostility to white America in response, with little action from Trump to make it worthwhile. The Biden administration began in fear of white Americans, while ending Trump's restrictions on entry from Muslim countries from which most terrorists came.

America would never again be great. America would never again be America.

When Twitter permanently suspended Trump's account, his more than sixty thousand tweets since 2009 disappeared from view. Actor Macaulay Culkin, whose girlfriend was Asian, supported calls to edit Trump out of his 1992 film *Home Alone 2*. Trump was vanishing as non-people did, in the communist tradition, without his most fervent supporters noticing.

However emboldened Trump's supporters felt amidst a mob one day, egged along by Trump, his opponents felt emboldened afterwards: lauding black nationalism, ready to lynch white nationalists where they found them. Because of its last weeks, Trump's presidency left America's poor and powerless more vulnerable than ever. From that vulnerability, the risks are greatest.

Trump might not care. It sometimes seemed that he would let America dissolve altogether if there was a headline in it about him.

The most optimistic view of Trump's presidency is that, much as others laid the groundwork for Trump's candidacy and presidency, Trump laid groundwork for a future administration to carry his promises into effect. That administration might be Republican, Democrat, or something else, but will have learned from Trump's success in 2016 and failure in 2020. Another president might make America great again.

President Clinton was receptive to American nationalism following Republicans' success in the Congressional elections of 1994. So was Senator Joe Biden.

From 2021, Trump might have made it difficult for Democrats to remain in their newfound disregard for poor and working-class Americans. He might have made it difficult for Republicans to return to theirs.

The extent to which Trump has lasting achievements from his presidency will depend upon the extent to which he and others infuse future administrations, Congress, and other American institutions with American nationalism: quietly cutting immigration, aiding American manufacturers, at least privately acknowledging Muslim terror. Not only white Americans want that.

Away from the hollering against Trump's rhetoric, a phenomenon little understood by white people played out. For the most part, other races do not like each other. It has nothing to do with white people. Other races have never liked each other.

Coming from cultures cognizant of race and religion, immigrants do not cease being cognizant by being around white Americans. In 2016 and 2020, there were immigrants supporting Trump: immigrants not wanting more immigrants.

Immigrants typically do not want immigrants from races other than their own. Chinese may well want more Chinese immigrants, but not more Koreans or Japanese. Indians do not want more Pakistanis. Africans do not want more Arabs. Immigrants doing well in white-majority America do not want other races dominating at their expense.

Might immigrants not want more immigrants even from their race, when those immigrants risk the lives they are building in America? Might immigrants making good homes not want sick, uneducated, and uneducable immigrants ruining America? Other races recognize crimes and social problems that white Americans refuse to understand. They might be less willing than white Americans to replicate in Boston the slums of Brazil.

Latinos are not the cultural monolith that white people welcoming them imagine them to be. Wealthy white Cubans whose families fled communism are unlike mixed-race Mexicans climbing over the border. Latinos not carrying Indian blood recognize the tribal and other implications of those who do.

In the Rio Grande Valley, south Texas, Tejanos are descended from Spanish settlers before Texas became part of America. They supported Trump.

"Today," Yvonne Trappe told *Politico* in November 2020, "the people coming over are not the kind of people who came before, like the braceros, who came to work, to educate their children, to better themselves." Braceros were Mexicans admitted to America for short periods to carry out seasonal agricultural work. "No, the people coming now are looking for handouts."

If Trump's presidency proves to have been successful, it will be because it began a process that Trump barely got underway. It will lead to others reviving American nationalism, not just among Republicans, but also among Democrats, libertarians, socialists, and everyone else. If Americans needing aid and defense do not get them from rich and powerful Americans, whether born to or acquiring riches and power, they will not get them from anyone.

There will always be choices come election time. America would be better served with two major political parties worth supporting than none, whatever their differences.

In such event, Trump could be accredited with raising the issues he raised in 2016 that no other Republican or Democrat presidential candidate raised. He could be credited with initiating a process that he did not fulfil in office, but that might not have taken place without him.

Trump was an observer, an inciter even. He was not a participant.

Achievement is hard. It cannot afford silly distractions.

A president who delivers what Trump failed to deliver will be a patriot and nationalist. He will have conviction in his country.

She will work hard in office. He will have integrity: telling the truth; honoring commitments. She will be practical, engaged with reality, wanting evidence before believing anything.

He will be calm and courteous, competent and well organized. She will collect and retain allies and supporters devoted to America. He will hire, retain, and promote nationalists on performance and loyalty to America, not to him personally.

She will not wantonly denigrate fellow Americans disagreeing with her. He will try to persuade them to his points of view.

Trump could have been the man who made America great again, had he honored his promises. Behaving as a nationalist, presiding as a nationalist, Trump could have become a figure of historical proportions.

Thus far, he is not. Ultimately, individualism is always self-destructive.

POSTSCRIPT: AUSTRALIA

In Australia, elections are held on Saturdays. Pre-poll voting is generally available for two or three weeks beforehand at select locations. Voting is compulsory. Only citizens can vote.

Independent federal, state, and territory electoral commissions conduct elections. They visit nursing homes, hospitals, and remote areas during each election period, to enable voting there.

They do not mail out ballot papers unsolicited, but only in response to applications for postal votes. They only issue ballot papers to people they know can vote, checked against each voter's name as if he or she stood at a polling booth. They initial each ballot paper issued, and know how many ballot papers are on issue. Postal voting generally favors conservative and incumbent candidates.

Elections must be fair and be seen to be fair. The High Court, sitting as the Court of Disputed Returns, ordered the Western Australian Senate election of 2013 be held again in 2014 because the number of ballot papers lost during the recount exceeded the margin for the election of the last two Senate seats.

In terms of rival leaders, the 1996 Australian federal election was much like the 2020 American presidential election. Schoolchildren rushed to see the incumbent Australian prime minister, in widely aired news footage.

In both elections, the incumbent enjoyed all the enthusiasm in the air, but was also arrogant, berating his critics and rivals. He did not appreciate the role of policy in his success at the preceding election, when he might have already been the most unpopular political figure in the country, but had the good fortune to face possibly the second most unpopular figure. He did not understand voters, seeming to have surrounded himself with people who deferred to him instead of aiding him with criticism that might have improved his leadership and election campaign.

The challenger enjoyed no enthusiasm, no adoring crowds. Nor did he inspire the hostility that the incumbent inspired.

Instead, the challenger had familiarity, from a long political career seeking the highest office in the land, never reaching it and often looking like he never would. Familiarity could be comforting, in an electorate tired of drama, that wanted politics to bore again. The challenger avoided policy differences between him and the incumbent, allowing the election to be much about personality.

The challenger, the nicer person, won. In Australia, he went onto a long and generally successful prime ministership, arguably the finest for half a century.

After the 1996 Australian election, the outgoing prime minister berated the Australian people for not understanding what he had been trying to do. After the 2020 American presidential election, Trump berated election officials, elected officials, judges, and anyone else for not believing that he won the election.

The difference might say something about the two men's different visions of themselves. The outgoing Australian prime minister saw himself as among the Western elites above the ordinary masses. Trump presented himself as being at war with the Western elites on behalf of the masses. He might have won re-election if he had been.

BIBLIOGRAPHY

Anonymous (Miles Taylor), *A Warning*, 2019.

Cheley, John, *Stories for Talks with Boys and Girls*, 1958.

Christie, Chris, *Let Me Finish: Trump, the Kushners, Bannon, New Jersey, and the Power of In-Your-Face Politics*, 2019.

Clinton, Hillary, *What Happened*, 2017.

Comey, James, *A Higher Loyalty: Truth, Lies and Leadership*, 2018.

Coulter, Ann, *¡Adios, America! The Left's Plan to Turn Our Country Into a Third World Hellhole*, 2015.

Coulter, Ann, *In Trump We Trust: E Pluribus Awesome!* 2016.

Green, Joshua, *Devil's Bargain: Steve Bannon, Donald Trump, and the Nationalist Uprising*, 2017.

Kurtz, Howard, *Media Madness: Donald Trump, the Press, and the War over the Truth*, 2018.

Leamer, Laurence, *Mar-a-Lago: Inside the Gates of Power at Donald Trump's Presidential Palace*, 2019.

Lysiak, Matthew, *The Drudge Revolution: The Untold Story of How Talk Radio, Fox News, and a Gift Shop Clerk with an Internet Connection Took Down the Mainstream Media*, 2020.

McCain, John, *The Restless Wave: Good Times, Just Causes, Great Fights, and Other Appreciations*, 2018.

Rucker, Philip and Leonnig, Carol, *A Very Stable Genius: Donald J. Trump's Testing of America*, 2020.

Trump, Ivana, *Raising Trump: Family Values from America's First Mother*, 2017.

Trump, Mary, *Too Much and Never Enough: How My Family Created the World's Most Dangerous Man*, 2020.

Wolff, Michael, *Fire and Fury: Inside the Trump White House*, 2018.

Wolkoff, Stephanie Winston, *Melania and Me: The Rise and Fall of My Friendship with the First Lady*, 2020.

Woodward, Bob, *Rage*, 2020.

Essays
Hugo, Victor, 'Villemain,' 1845.

SELECTED REFERENCES

Anonymous (Miles Taylor), 'I Am Part of the Resistance Inside the Trump Administration,' *The New York Times* newspaper, 5 September 2018.

Baker, Peter and others, 'Jared Kushner and Ivanka Trump: Pillars of Family-Driven West Wing,' *The New York Times* newspaper, 15 April 2017.

Barber, Lionel and others, 'Donald Trump: Without Twitter, I would not be here — FT interview,' *Financial Times* newspaper, 3 April 2017.

Budryk, Zack, 'Deportations lower under Trump administration than Obama: report,' *The Hill*, 18 November 2019.

Carrasquillo, Adrian, 'Steve Bannon Detonates His Trump Survival Plan, Worrying Allies,' *Buzz Feed News*, 17 August 2017.

Cathey, Libby, 'Trump, downplaying virus, has mocked wearing masks for months,' *ABC News*, 3 October 2020.

Chen, Shawna, 'Donald Trump, Expert,' *Politico*, 3 September 2019.

Colvin, Jill and another, 'Trump signs immigration order featuring numerous exemptions,' *Associated Press* news service, 23 April 2020.

Dawsey, Josh and another, 'Trump's got a new favorite Steve,' referring to Stephen Miller, *Politico*, 13 April 2017.

Dockterman, Eliana, 'President Trump's Inauguration Crowd Doesn't Look Like Barack Obama's Did in 2009,' *Time* magazine, 20 January 2017.

Drucker, David, ''I feel bad that I left': John Kelly warned Trump he would be impeached,' *Washington Examiner* magazine, 26 October 2019.

Fahrenthold, David, 'Trump recorded having extremely lewd conversation about women in 2005,' *The Washington Post* newspaper, 8 October 2016.

Fahrenthold, David and others, 'Ballrooms, candles and luxury cottages: During Trump's term, millions of government and GOP dollars have flowed to his properties,' *The Washington Post* newspaper, 27 October 2020.

Fellman, Gordon, 'Jared Kushner and Stephen Miller Are the Most Assimilated Jews in America,' *Haaretz* newspaper, 21 December 2018.

Frenkel, Sheera and another, ''A Total Failure': The Proud Boys Now Mock Trump,' *The New York Times* newspaper, 20 January 2021.

Giaritelli, Anna, 'Trump has not built a single mile of new border fence after 30 months in office,' *Washington Examiner* magazine, 20 July 2019.

Gold, Matea, 'The campaign to impeach President Trump has begun,' *The*

Washington Post newspaper, 21 January 2017.

Goodnough, Abby and another, 'The Elderly vs. Essential Workers: Who Should Get the Coronavirus Vaccine First?' *The New York Times* newspaper, 5 December 2020.

Haberman, Maggie and others, 'In Battle for Trump's Heart and Mind, It's Bannon vs. Kushner,' *The New York Times* newspaper, 6 April 2017.

Hauslohner, Abigail, 'The Trump administration's immigration jails are packed, but deportations are lower than in Obama era,' *The Washington Post* newspaper, 18 November 2019.

Herrera, Jack, 'Trump Didn't Win the Latino Vote in Texas. He Won the Tejano Vote,' *Politico*, 17 November 2020.

Hunter, Derek, 'Coulter Unloads: 'A Joke Presidency' That 'Scammed The American People' With Promises Of A Wall,' *Daily Caller*, 19 December 2018.

Isenstadt, Alex, 'Trump pollster's campaign autopsy paints damning picture of defeat,' *Politico*, 1 February 2021.

Johnson, Simon, 'Eric Trump: Nepotism is a 'beautiful thing' as he says US President's children are more likely to speak truth to power,' *The Daily Telegraph* newspaper, 10 April 2017.

Kai, Wang, 'I'm not a virus: Chinese man gets warm hugs in Florence,' *China News Service*, 5 February 2020.

Karni, Annie and another, 'Ivanka Trump Now Acknowledges: 'I'm a Proud Trump Republican',' *The New York Times* newspaper, 2 March 2020.

Kaufmann, Eric, 'Trumpism is here to stay,' *UnHerd*, 18 January 2021.

Keith, Tamara and others, 'How 15 Days Became 45: Trump Extends Guidelines To Slow Coronavirus,' *NPR*, 30 March 2020.

Kim, Soo, 'Cuomo Calls New York's COVID-19 Response 'Beautiful' As Nearly 1 in 5 Deaths From State,' *Newsweek* magazine, 18 August 2020.

Kim, Tae, 'Indefensible: Hedge fund tax loophole shows 'swamp' still rules over Washington, D.C.,' *CNBC*, 21 December 2017.

Klemesrud, Judy, 'Donald Trump, Real Estate Promoter, Builds Image as He Buys Buildings,' *The New York Times* newspaper, 1 November 1976.

Kohn, Sally, 'The Old White Man's Last Hurrah,' *Time* magazine, 29 February 2016.

Korecki, Natasha and others, 'Inside Donald Trump's 2020 undoing,' *Politico*, 7 November 2020.

Kristol, William, 'It Came Apart: What's Next for a Fractured Culture,' *American Enterprise Institute* channel, You Tube, 8 February 2017.

Kristol, William, 'It's Our War, Bush should go to Jerusalem — and the U.S. should confront Iran,' *Weekly Standard* magazine, 24 July 2006.

Lemire, Jonathan and another, 'Virus, racial unrest force Trump campaign to recalibrate,' *Associated Press*, 8 June 2020.

Maraniss, David, 'Lessons of Humbling Loss Guide Clinton's Journey,'

The Washington Post newspaper, 14 July 1992.

Mardell, Mark, 'Meet the First Son-in-Law,' transcribed as 'Jared Kushner: Who is the Trump whisperer?' *The World This Weekend*, BBC Radio 4, 24 April 2017.

Miller, Claire Cain and others, 'Meet the Supporters Trump Has Lost,' *The New York Times* newspaper, 1 July 2020.

Nichols, Tom, 'This Republican Party Is Not Worth Saving,' *The Atlantic* magazine, 10 September 2020.

Noonan, Peggy, 'The Week It Went South for Trump,' *The Wall Street Journal*, 25 June 2020.

Parker, Ashley, 'Karen Pence is the vice president's 'prayer warrior,' gut check and shield,' *The Washington Post* newspaper, 28 March 2017.

Peters, Jeremy, 'The 'Never Trump' Coalition That Decided Eh, Never Mind, He's Fine,' *The New York Times* newspaper, 5 October 2019.

Peters, Jeremy and another, 'Trump Undercuts Bannon, Whose Job May Be in Danger,' *The New York Times* newspaper, 12 April 2017.

Samuels, Brett, 'Trump denies 'mini-strokes' sent him to Walter Reed,' *The Hill*, 1 September 2020.

Scheer, Robert, 'Dinner With Drudge,' USC Annenberg *Online Journalism Review*, 16 July 1998.

Sen, Sandip, 'How China locked down internally for COVID-19, but pushed foreign travel,' *The Economic Times* newspaper, 30 April 2020.

Sherman, Gabriel, 'The Legacy,' referring to Jared Kushner, *New York* magazine, 10 July 2009.

Shumei, Leng and another, 'US urged to release health info of military athletes who came to Wuhan in October 2019,' *Global Times* newspaper, 25 March 2020.

Silver, Nate, 'Election Update: Where Are the Undecided Voters?' *Five Thirty Eight*, 25 October 2016.

Smalley, Suzanne, 'Ann Coulter doesn't know if she will vote for 'defective man' Donald Trump,' *Yahoo News*, 28 May 2020.

Solomon, Feliz, 'Hillary Clinton Called for Strikes on Syrian Airfields Shortly Before Trump's Announcement,' *Time* magazine, 7 April 2017.

Thompson, Dennis, 'What You Need to Know Now About the Wuhan Virus,' *Health Day News*, 23 January 2020.

Tucker, Jill, 'Abraham Lincoln, once a hero, is now a bad guy in some S.F. education circles,' *San Francisco Chronicle* newspaper, 14 December 2020.

Vogl, Anthea, 'There's a ban on leaving Australia under COVID-19. Who can get an exemption to go overseas? And how?' *The Conversation*, 31 August 2020.

Webel, Mari, 'Calling COVID-19 a 'Chinese virus' is wrong and dangerous – the pandemic is global,' *The Conversation*, 25 March 2020.

Dates after 1996 are Internet dates. Print dates are generally a day later.

INDEX

ABOUT THE AUTHOR

Simon Lennon has lived, worked, and traveled throughout America, Europe, Australasia, Asia, and the South Pacific. He has university bachelor's degrees in science and law and university master's degrees in commerce and business.

He has been a member of the same political party since 1988. He is married with six children.

Short Story Collections
Gender in America
Discovering Race

Novels
The King of a Vacant City
Swansong of a Childless People
A Young Man's Tale
The Insubordinate
Mahmood and Mrs Wynworth

Non-Fiction
The Unnatural West: An Overview
The Tribeless West: An Overview
The Homeless West: An Overview
The Vanishing West: An Overview
Western Individualism
The End of Natural Selection
The Need for Nations
People's Identity: Race and Racism
Of Whom We're Born: Race and Family
Biological Us: Gender and Sexuality
A Land to Belong: Nationalism
The Failure of Multiculturalism
Reclaiming Western Cultures
Christendom Lost
Aiding Islam
The Individualism of Donald Trump

www.ingramcontent.com/pod-product-compliance
Lightning Source LLC
Chambersburg PA
CBHW030836090426
42737CB00009B/989